BOLSHEVISM, FASCISM, AND CAPITALISM

BOLSHEVISM, FASCISM, AND CAPITALISM

AN ACCOUNT OF THE THREE ECONOMIC SYSTEMS

BY

GEORGE S. COUNTS
LUIGI VILLARI
MALCOLM C. RORTY
NEWTON D. BAKER

Essay Index Reprint Series

BOOKS FOR LIBRARIES PRESS
FREEPORT, NEW YORK

HP 82

B 56

1970

~~330.1~~

~~B693~~

INTERNATIONAL STANDARD BOOK NUMBER:

0-8369-1866-5

LIBRARY OF CONGRESS CATALOG CARD NUMBER:

71-128211

PRINTED IN THE UNITED STATES OF AMERICA

CONTENTS

THE SOVIET PLANNING SYSTEM AND THE FIVE-YEAR PLAN

BY GEORGE S. COUNTS

THE SOVIET PLANNING SYSTEM AND THE FIVE-YEAR PLAN

I

ALTHOUGH many observers profess to see signs of good omen in the economic skies, as they have daily during the past two years, the economic depression continues to hold the entire western world in its grip, depriving millions of men of employment and bringing misery to vast populations. In spite of the fact that we in America possess an abundance of natural resources and a mastery over the forces of production that should enable us to satisfy all of our material wants with ease, multitudes go hungry and experience all the terrors and humiliations of profound physical insecurity. Apparently, nothing short of a miracle can save us from one of the most terrible winters of our history. This is tragedy; not because men have not suffered before, but because they now suffer so needlessly. The dreams of mankind through the ages are at last capable of realization, but our present economic, political, and educational leadership has thus far failed to rise to the opportunity created by science and technology. A general condition of incoördination ·paralyzes the economic system and dissipates its matchless energies. It is apparently this situation which is turning the minds of our generation to a consideration of the question of social planning.

The growing interest in social planning, however, is not to be traced entirely to the depression. Another factor is found in the numerous experiments looking toward the coördination of the various aspects of the economic life which are under way in the world. And there is one experiment in this realm that dwarfs all others—so bold, indeed, in its ideals and its program that few contemplate it without emotion. Even today, almost fourteen years after the Bolshevik revolution, the Soviet experiment is so enveloped with the clouds of passion that we have great difficulty in gaining a clear picture of the new structure which is rapidly taking form. While generations will have to come and go before that experiment can be accurately appraised in all of its details, quite possibly its most revolutionary feature will be found in its planning system. Whatever else Soviet Russia may be doing, she is endeavoring with all the resources at her command to bring the economic order under some measure of rational control in the interests of the masses.

Whether this effort proves successful or not, it merits the most careful study. Moreover, if such study is to be profitable, it should be entirely fair, and even generous. We shall gain nothing by regarding everything that comes out of the Soviet Union as propaganda and by steadfastly closing our ears to unpleasant facts. We should even drop the condescending manner which we are accustomed to assume whenever we contemplate Russian achievements. This, of course, is asking a great deal, when we remember how often in history the representatives of a culture which for the moment is dominant have thought themselves unable to learn from the representatives of another. Also, we should find little satisfaction in stating ponderously and with finality that the Soviet experiment violates the

known laws of human nature, comfortably assuming
that our own institutions are in perfect harmony
with those laws. As a matter of fact, in our reflections upon human nature we can add but little to the
dictum of John Adams to the effect that food and
sex are the great primary human urges. Apparently,
man is capable of adjusting himself to almost any
set of social arrangements conceivable. My belief in
this principle has been greatly strengthened during
the past four years as I have seen millions of my
fellow citizens living and apparently enjoying themselves in the city of New York. A race of men that
refuses to fly from the subways, the streets, the
dwellings, the haste, and the noise of this great
metropolis is obviously equipped by nature to endure anything.

Most of us no doubt heard of the Five-Year Plan
before we had heard of the Soviet planning system.
The latter, however, is far more important than the
former, because it produced the Five-Year Plan and
is capable of producing many more. Indeed, it has
already given birth to a number of plans and is now
busy hatching others. The time is consequently not
far distant when we shall cease speaking of *the*
Five-Year Plan and begin to speak of the first, second, or third five-year plan. This is a matter which
it is well to understand. Otherwise we shall miss the
central fact in the Soviet experiment. That experiment is characterized by the introduction of the idea
of planning into the social structure. Soviet society
is now equipped to plan its future as our society is
equipped to maintain order or educate its children.

Our examination of the Soviet program of planning will be divided into two parts. In the first we

shall confine ourselves to a description of the system of planning organs, an outline of the major purposes and provisions of the Five-Year Plan, and a report on the fortunes of the plan to date. In the second an effort will be made to appraise the Soviet experiment in planning, assess its points of strength and weakness, and speculate somewhat with respect to the future. I shall endeavor to limit the presentation of statistical data to the narrowest possible proportions. The statistics of the Five-Year Plan may be found in any one of a dozen or more reliable references.

The actual planning of economic services has marched hand in hand with the socialization of the various branches of the public economy. During the early years of the revolution the planning was done by the Government itself. But as the magnitude of the work increased and as its importance came to be recognized, the necessity of delegating this function to some specially created agency became increasingly apparent. The result was the founding of the Gosplan or State Planning Commission on February 22, 1921. This institution was not born in a fully developed form. In fact it has been changing and growing from the very day of its birth; and even now at the age of ten years no one would be so bold as to endeavor to forecast its form at the time of maturity. Already, however, it has begun to play a central rôle in the building of the new society and to react vigorously upon the revolutionary forces which brought it into existence.

Before examining the State Planning Commission itself, let us indicate its position in the Soviet governmental system. The supreme organ of authority in the country is the All-Union Congress of Soviets which meets for a few weeks at least once every two years. During the interval between congresses power rests with the Central Executive Committee which is composed of something less than six hundred members. But, since this body is not in continuous session, meeting only three times a year, the actual responsibilities of government are generally discharged by the Presidium of the Committee. The executive arm of the Presidium is the Council of People's Commissars which embraces the heads of all governmental departments and corresponds roughly in function to the President's Cabinet in the United States. One of the most important organs of the Council of People's Commissars is the State Planning Commission. It should, of course, not be forgotten that back of and permeating these various organs of government is the real ruling power of Soviet Russia—the Communist party.

In its structure the State Planning Commission is extremely complex. Any description is likely, therefore, to convey a false impression of simplicity. Even a diagram representing its various parts and its relationships to the other organs of the Soviet state contributes but little to understanding. Yet a few general remarks concerning its nature will serve to clear up certain misconceptions which seem to prevail generally in the United States. The common notion that the Commission consists of a dozen or so economists who sit in their swivel chairs in Moscow and conjure out of the air elaborate plans for the economic development of the Union seems to have little basis in fact. The reality presents an entirely different picture.

The planning organs of Soviet Russia constitute a vast system which reaches from Moscow to the most remote corners and the most retarded cultures of the country. There is, to be sure, an All-Union Planning Commission with offices in Moscow. But there is also a planning commission in each of the seven constituent republics comprising the Union, a planning commission in each of the more important of the thirty so-called autonomous republics and areas, a planning commission in each of the great *oblasts* into which a republic is ordinarily divided, and even planning commissions in the yet smaller politico-economic divisions. Very commonly, too, there are planning bodies associated with the more important divisions or departments of government, industry, and culture.

These various commissions sustain intimate relationships with the appropriate soviets, with the Communist party, with the different trade-unions, with the various commissariats, with the great economic trusts, and with other organs of the social structure. Then they are welded together into a single instrument and made to constitute a comprehensive and complex system which is devoted to social planning, just as the schools are devoted to education or the police force to the maintenance of order.

An examination of the organization of the central commission in Moscow will give a general idea of the functions which the planning system is expected to discharge. Except for a few unimportant qualifications the institution may be said to be divided into four great departments. The first department is concerned with the basic problems of the planning of production and the allocation of capital in the various divisions of the economy. This department is subdivided into appropriate sections, such as transport, agriculture, manufacture, mining, chemistry, and lumbering. The second department is responsible for the gathering of statistics, the keeping of accounts, and the study of business trends at home and throughout the world. The third department is supposed to discharge the crucial function of discovering defects in the economic order and of advancing the technical level of the entire productive system. The fourth department embraces the important domains of labor, culture, and science. Its central function is to transmute gains in economic efficiency into the achievement of the great social and cultural purposes in whose name the revolutionary struggle has been waged. The hope is that mastery over economic processes will be attended not by a struggle for ever larger markets but rather by a concerted attempt to enrich the spiritual life of the masses.

In general, the subsidiary planning commissions in the different republics and in the smaller divisions of the Union are similar in structure and function to the central commission in the capital city. Each possesses certain characteristics which are peculiar to itself and which reflect the condition of industry and culture in its particular area. But everywhere the planning organs are dealing with the same fundamental problems: They are gathering data from life and bringing these data to bear on the numerous tasks of planning and of organizing the entire social economy in the light of the ideals of the revolution. Being closely integrated into a single system, they provide the means for the general pooling of knowledge and for the focusing of experience on the surmounting of any obstacle.

The formulation of a general plan for the economic and cultural development of the Union is an extremely complicated and arduous undertaking. It involves the coördination of the activities of all the different elements and divisions of the planning system and of numerous related institutions besides; it involves the enlistment of the energies of the entire body of self-conscious and revolutionary-minded workers in the country; it involves innumerable conferences, meetings, and discussions. Thus, during the months of December, 1927, and January, 1928, when the foundations of the Five-Year Plan were being laid, there were held sixteen All-Union conferences, as well as numerous smaller conferences, on various phases of the plan. And after a plan is launched the Commission keeps a careful and continuous record of its operation and modifies its provisions in the light of experience.

The total process of planning, however, is not carried on within the organs of the State Planning Commission. They merely develop the general plan. There then remains the task of making the plan concrete and of relating it to the actual conditions of life. This is the function of the several commissariats whose areas of jurisdiction fall within the scope of the plan. So the Commissariats of Agriculture, of Transport, of Posts and Telegraph, of Labor, of Trade and Commerce, of Finance, of Education, of Health, and of Social Welfare all develop their own detailed programs for the realization of the general plan. The way in which this is done may be illustrated by reference to the work of the Supreme Economic Council.

In the realization of any comprehensive plan for the development of the public economy, the Supreme Economic Council probably bears heavier responsibilities than any other department of the Government. In position and function it is coördinate with the various commissariats and has general charge of all branches of industry: coal, oil, metal, electrical, chemical, timber, paper, textile, silicate, food, leather, and others. In order that the Council may discharge its heavy duties effectively, all the industries of the Union, except those which are still in the stage of handicrafts, are organized into some sixty great trusts and a considerable number of less powerful economic units. Through these trusts the Supreme Economic Council endeavors to stimulate, coördinate, and regulate the expansion of Soviet industry as a whole.

Also by means of the trusts the Council translates the general plan into concrete and specific terms. It thus develops a plan of its own known as the *promfinplan* (industrial financial plan) which embraces all branches of industry and every factory, mill, and mine in the Union. During the earlier days of planning, and down almost to the close of the second year of the Five-Year Plan, the *promfinplan* was formulated for the most part from the top and imposed upon each particular establishment. But in the months of September and October and November of 1930 certain fundamental changes occurred which seem to be having considerable effect on the processes of planning. As a product of a stirring campaign carried on among the rank and file to speed up the program of production and achieve the plan in four years, the workers, first in a few plants and later everywhere, assumed responsibilities for planning. They now take the *promfinplan* of the Council, test it against their experience, and suggest the appropriate revision. The resultant plan has been christened the *fstretchny promfinplan* and is commonly regarded as a significant addition to the technique of planning. The Russian adjective practically defies translation. We can only say that it designates a process which goes from the bottom upward, from the point of production through the successive levels of management, and establishes indices for the year on the basis of the actual accomplishments of the better workmen. During the short period of its existence it seems to have served in stimulating the interest of labor in the program and in raising the tempo of production.

The actual functioning of the State Planning Commission may be best illustrated by examining the Five-Year Plan. Although the Commission has formulated an annual plan in the so-called control figures of industry every year since 1925 and has organized several more elaborate projects, the great plan launched in October, 1928, is by far its most ambitious achievement and the most gigantic program of construction ever undertaken by any government. Already it is opening up new perspectives of development, releasing the energies of the masses, and even changing the psychology of the people in ways that could not have been anticipated. If the plan is successful it will not only greatly alter the internal situation but will also radically affect the position of the Soviet Union in the family of nations. It should likewise strengthen the status and quicken the spread of the revolutionary movement in the less prosperous countries of the world.

As first developed the plan took the form of two variants: the one was called the minimal and the other the maximal variant. The first was based upon the assumption that crops would be poor, that credits would not be forthcoming from capitalistic countries, that the difficulties of securing satisfactory conditions for construction would exceed the anticipation, and that a relatively large proportion of the income would have to be diverted to purposes of defense. The second took a somewhat more optimistic view of the future. It assumed good harvests throughout the five-year period, an improvement in the relations with the world economic order, an acute rise in the quality of the conditions affecting construction, and an appreciable reduction in the proportion of the income required for military purposes.

The fact should be emphasized, however, that in their fundamental positions the two variants were not to be distinguished. They both provided for the industrialization of the country and the collectivization of agriculture. Likewise, the distribution of the public income in general and the share of the income going to the proletariat in particular were approximately identical in both variants. They differed merely in the rate of development contemplated. The minimal variant may therefore be regarded as a small edition of the maximal variant. Thus, the program, which under the conditions anticipated in the maximal variant would be completed in five

years, would require about six years if the less favorable conditions should prevail.

When the two variants were finally brought before the Party and the Government for consideration, it was the maximal and not the minimal program that was approved. The data to be given
subsequently in this lecture are therefore drawn altogether from the more ambitious variant. The minimal variant would seem to be a matter of interest
only for the historian.

Running through the Five-Year Plan like the
themes of an opera are two fundamental purposes.
The first is the rapid industrialization of the country; and the second is the radical socialistic reconstruction of the village. While the plan embraces
many other important objectives, these two purposes constitute its essence.

The interest of the Soviet leaders in industrialization is easily understood. Because of the difficulties
which they have faced in their relationships with
capitalistic countries and which they think are likely
to continue, they have concluded that the guarding
of the revolution itself is dependent on the development of industry. They feel an especial concern over
the establishment of the so-called heavy industries—
the industries which produce not the objects of use
but the tools of production. Without such industries
they fear that in the course of time the Soviet Union
would gradually fall into the position of an agrarian
colony of western capitalism. They also realize that
in case of military conflict victory must ordinarily
go to the nation which is best equipped to produce
the materials and engines of war. In the modern
world only an industrial nation can survive.

But there is an even more fundamental reason for this eagerness to build factories and mills and railroads and electric stations. The Soviet leaders believe that the attitude of mind which is indispensable for the construction of a socialistic state appears only under the conditions of industrialism. In support of this thesis they often quote the following words from Lenin:

To suppose that all who toil are equally gifted for this task [of building socialism] would be the emptiest phrase or illusion of the antediluvian, pre-Marxian socialist; because this ability does not create itself but grows historically and grows only out of large capitalistic production. Only the proletariat on its march from capitalism to socialism possesses this ability.

Thus, in their program of industrialization, they are seeking not only to erect a defense against foreign capitalism but also to destroy those individualistic tendencies which thrive on private property and small-scale production.

The socialistic reconstruction of the village may be regarded as the other side of the same question. So long as the Soviet Union remains preponderantly rural and the rural population follows an individualistic economy, the building of a socialistic state is impossible. Under such conditions society will always be divided and the weight of numbers will be on the side of capitalism. In the Five-Year Plan the Communists have gone to the root of the matter, attacked the enemy in his own stronghold, and initiated a program which is designed to change radically not only the form of agricultural production but even the very temper of the rural population.

This battle over the soil which was precipitated by the launching of the plan is certainly one of the most crucial battles in history.

There were also sound economic reasons for the collectivization of agriculture. Following the revolution the great estates were broken up and the number of peasant households increased from about seventeen million to twenty-six million. This division of the land, combined with the use of the strip system, produced as inefficient a form of agricultural economy as could well be imagined. The use of modern farm machinery was made impossible, much land was removed from cultivation, and production fell off. There were but two possible courses of action. In the first place, the Government might lend its support to the rich peasants, stimulate the growth of private enterprise, and thus insure the desired increase in production. In the second place, it might ally itself with the poor and middle peasantry, break the power of the *kulak,* organize collective and state farms, and modernize the forms of agricultural production. To a socialist or communist government there was of course no choice. The collectivization of the village was the only defensible course.

Contrary to the common opinion held in America the Five-Year Plan is not merely an economic plan. It also has important social and cultural divisions. In this lecture it will be possible only to mention the more important provisions of the maximum variant of the plan as originally formulated.

On the economic side the plan called for an increase of production in all state industry of 180 per cent; an increase in heavy industry of 230 per cent and in light industry of 144 per cent; an advance in the production of electricity from five billion to twenty-two billion kilowatt hours annually; a growth in oil production from eleven million to twenty-two million tons; an increase in coal production from thirty-five million to seventy-five million tons; a growth in the production of pig iron from four million to ten million tons; a fourfold advance in machine production; an advance in the production of chemical fertilizer from four hundred thousand to eight million tons; a 56 per cent increase in agricultural production; a growth of 22 per cent in the land brought under cultivation; the bringing of six million peasant households into collective farms totaling sixty-five million acres; the putting of ten billion rubles into transport during the five years; the building of seventeen thousand kilometers of railroad; an increase in the number of automobiles from twenty-five thousand to more than three hundred thousand; the drawing into the public economy of agricultural, timber, fuel, and metal resources of vast areas in the Transvolga, the Urals, Kazakstan, Siberia, Transcaucasia, and the Far East; the reduction of the cost of industrial production by 35 per cent during the five years; the increase in the productivity of labor by 110 per cent; and the putting into all kinds of public construction between 1928 and 1933 of sixty-five billion rubles.

On the social and cultural side the plan contemplated the full extension of the seven-hour working day to all industrial and transport workers; the raising of nominal wages by 47 per cent and of real wages by 71 per cent; the reduction of the number of unemployed by more than 50 per cent; a large increase in medical facilities and institutions; the growth of the expenditure on social insurance from 967 million rubles to 1,950 million rubles annually; the teaching of eighteen million persons between the ages of eighteen and thirty-five to read and write; the introduction of universal primary education throughout practically the entire Union by 1932–33; the increase of the number of libraries from approximately twenty-three thousand to thirty-four thousand; the radical expansion of the cinema, the radio, the press, the post, the telegraph, and all forms of adult education; the promotion of the rapid development of secondary, technical, higher, and continuation schools; the training of almost two million workers for industry, transport, and construction; the giving to five million peasants of the elements of agricultural knowledge; the preparation of two hundred thousand tractorists and fifty thousand mechanics for the farms; the training of sixty thousand engineers and one hundred and twenty thousand technicians; the preparation of fifty thousand specialists of middle and higher qualification for agriculture; the training of fifty-six thousand teachers of higher and one hundred and sixty-four thousand of lower qualification; the preparation of eighteen thousand physicians and forty thousand medical and pharmaceutical personnel of middle qualification; the training of great numbers of other specialists for the various branches of the public economy; and generally the reorganization of the entire system of vocational, technical, and professional training.

In the light of the technical and cultural backwardness of the country and in view of the exhausting efforts called forth by war, revolution, and famine, the Five-Year Plan is truly, as the Soviet leaders commonly say, "a program of great works." It calls for the coördinated development of a country of limitless resources embracing almost one-sixth of the land surface of the globe and inhabited by approximately one hundred and sixty million people. It would seem to be no exaggeration to characterize it as the greatest social experiment of all time. What then have been the fortunes of the plan? And will it succeed? To summarize in a few words the achievements of so vast an undertaking is of course impossible. I shall therefore merely endeavor to record the major successes and failures and indicate their significance.

The successes of the first year were striking. In the total production of large state industry the plan had called for an increase over the preceding twelve months of 21.4 per cent; the actual achievement was 23.4 per cent; and the control figure for the following year was raised to 31.5 per cent. Also the plan was equaled or surpassed in the important fields of capital construction, transportation of freight, number of employed workers, average monthly wage, length of working day and total state income. In the realm of the socialization of agriculture the plan was likewise exceeded. The number of acres brought under some form of collectivization by October, 1929, was 11.8 million in place of the 9.3 million called for by the plan.

On the other side of the ledger, however, were recorded certain serious failures. Increased production in the textile, leather, rubber, and shoe industries, for example, was attended not by an improvement but by a depreciation in the quality of the product. The lowering of the costs of production also did not proceed according to schedule, although advances over the previous year were general all along the line. No doubt this was due in part to the fact that the productivity of labor did not increase as rapidly as contemplated. The plan had called for an advance of 17 per cent, whereas the actual achievement was only 15 per cent. But the most serious gaps between program and accomplishment were in the field of agriculture. The total production was expected to increase 4.4 per cent, but a growth of only 1.8 per cent was registered. The amount of cultivated land missed the mark set by 3 per cent. On the other hand, the quantity of agricultural produce to reach the markets of the country somewhat surpassed the expectation.

Because of the successes of this year the control figures for the second year were raised above the provisions of the original maximum variant of the plan at many points and the Communists began to talk of achieving the plan in four or four and one-half years. This practice of formulating control figures every year has led to much confusion in the minds of foreign reporters and observers, if not in the minds of large numbers of Soviet citizens themselves. With the passage of the years it becomes increasingly difficult to know just what the Five-Year Plan is, whether it is to be found in the first formulation or in the revised or re-revised figures.

The second year was filled with drama and excitement. The revolutionary forces seemed, on the one hand, to score the most extraordinary triumphs and, on the other, to experience the most severe reverses.

The reader of the Soviet press must have begun to doubt his own sanity, for he would be told in the same issue of a paper that the plan would be achieved in four years and that the program was lagging everywhere. So much concrete evidence of failure was reported from day to day that the hostile critic would have had no difficulty in proving the imminent collapse of the entire experiment. That dispatches appearing in the American press alternately gave the impression that the Soviet Government was about to fall and that Soviet industry would shortly capture the markets of the world may be easily understood. As a matter of fact, these dispatches reflected the strategy of the Communist leaders as much as the ebb and flow of the struggle to fulfil the plan. Confusion was also often due to the failure to distinguish between the provisions of the original plan and the control figures for the year.

Besides numerous other achievements, the twelve months from October, 1929, to October, 1930, witness the movement for the collectivization of agriculture sweeping like a tidal wave through the villages of the Soviet Union; the practical liquidation of the *kulak* as a class and the general strengthening of the revolutionary forces among the peasants; the completion more than a year ahead of the original schedule of the Turkestan-Siberian railroad, linking together two great regions and opening up vast new areas for settlement; the breaking of ground for the Ford automobile factory near Nizhni Novgorod, and the beginning of work on numerous industrial enterprises in different parts of the country; the resumption of the export of grain on a large scale, and the marked increase in the amount of

timber, coal, oil, and other products sent into the
foreign market; the practical abolition of unemployment among persons possessing any special
knowledge or skill; and the laying of plans for the
introduction of universal primary education approximately two and one-half years ahead of the
plan as first formed.

This, however, is by no means the whole of the
story. These same twelve months recorded the
wholesale slaughtering of domestic animals by de-
spairing peasants who felt themselves being driven
into communal arrangements; the gross mismanagement of the great tractor factory just completed in
Stalingrad and of other important units in the new
industrial order; the growing inadequacy of the system of transportation to meet the heavy demands
made upon it; the restless movement of workers
from factory to factory and from industry back to
village; the marked tendency toward the inflation of
the ruble and the hoarding of metal coins; the increasing scarcity of all kinds of food and manufactured goods and the general lowering of the standard of living of urban dwellers; the extension of the
rationing system and the lengthening of the queues
in the cities; the growing alarm in Europe and
America over the effect of Soviet exports on the
markets of the world; the rapid reduction of prices
received for exports because of the spread of the
economic depression; and, finally, and perhaps most
serious of all, a marked slowing down of production
all along the line during July, August, and September.

A dispassionate analysis of the work of the second year reveals a very uneven advance along the

front of construction. In the department of agriculture the successes were so marked as to become almost embarrassing. During the winter of 1929–30, under the slogan of *The Liquidation of the Kulak as a Class,* the campaign for collectivization gained the momentum and generally took on the features of a mob movement. It went far beyond the facts of peasant psychology and rolled up such huge totals from week to week that some enthusiasts envisaged the complete collectivization of agriculture during the year.

Certain by-products of this drive to reconstruct the village were the sharpening of the class struggle among the peasants, the intensification of the campaign against religion, and the general shifting of the revolutionary front from the city to the country. When, following Stalin's famous letter to the press on the second of March entitled "Dizziness from Success," which sought to restore sanity among the organizers and promoters of this work, the smoke of battle had cleared away and the process of de-collectivization had run its course, it was found that the Five-Year Plan had already been surpassed and that eighty-five million acres had been brought into the collective farms. This meant not far from 25 per cent of the total cultivated area, whereas the plan called for but 20 per cent by 1933. At the same time the land brought into the great state farms grew to more than ten million acres. As a result of these changes in the conduct of agriculture the area under cultivation was increased by approximately 10 per cent and the total production by about 20 per cent. The second year of the plan consequently, in all probability, saw the emergence of a new form of agricultural production in the Soviet Union.

In the field of industrial production the developments of the second year were somewhat less spectacular than in the realm of agriculture. Although the plan, as originally outlined in its maximum variant, was slightly surpassed, the revised figures were not reached. The plan called for an increase of 21.5 per cent, the control figures for an increase of 31.5 per cent, and the actual accomplishment was an increase of 24.2 per cent over the previous year. This meant that the total output of industry in 1929–30 was approximately double that of 1913. In the case of coal production the increase for the second year was 17.6 per cent as against 13.4 per cent according to the plan. Corresponding percentages for oil were 26.0 and 12.1; for pig iron, 24.0 and 22.0; and for rolled steel, 14.5 and 11.1. The control figures for the year were exceeded in oil, paper, leather, and certain other branches, whereas they were not achieved in the coal, chemical, and metallurgical industries. The outlay for capital construction in industry amounted to 3.73 billion rubles in place of the 2.33 billion provided by the plan.

While these achievements were unquestionably remarkable, they failed to reach the level set by the control figures for the second year. This was due chiefly to the fact that the industrial program slowed down perceptibly during the last quarter of the year. Various incoördinations appeared in the public economy; but perhaps a yet more important factor contributing to the reduction of efficiency was the lowered morale of labor occasioned by mismanagement in the distribution of food and other commodities. This led to the migration of tens of thousands of workers from place to place in search of better conditions. Great numbers who were still peasants in spirit returned to their homes in the village in order to partake of the abundant harvest.

The most serious difficulties, however, occurred precisely where they had appeared during the first year. Quality failed to keep pace with quantity. Many plants reported increases in the amount of trash and inferior goods produced. The productivity of labor also refused to advance according to the plan, and the reduction of costs continued to lag grievously. Thus, whereas the plan called for an 11 per cent lowering of the costs of production, the actual achievement reached a scant 6 per cent. These facts were undoubtedly largely responsible for the marked depreciation of the ruble.

The cultural program scored numerous successes during the second year. There was a marked expansion of all institutions devoted to the preparation of skilled workers, technicians, and engineers; the expenditures on popular education passed well beyond a billion dollars, as compared with 738 million for the previous year; the number of pupils in public schools grew from 11,914,500 to 13,500,000 within the course of the twelve months; and preparations were made for the introduction of universal compulsory education in the first grade of the primary school during the early part of 1931. The year likewise witnessed large achievements in the attack on illiteracy, in the publication of books, in the spread of libraries and reading rooms, in the widening of the network of cinema and radio stations, and in the extension of medical facilities to the population.

With the close of the second year of the plan the economic year was made identical with the calendar year. As a consequence, October, November, and December of 1930 were designated as a special *shock* quarter. At the same time the control figures for the third year were raised to fantastic heights. Thus, according to this revision of the plan, industrial production was to grow during the year by 52 per cent, heavy industry by 62 per cent, and light industry by 37 per cent. In the case of agriculture the total seeded area was to increase by 12 per cent, the collective farms by 20 per cent, and the state farms by 50 per cent. Similar advances were contemplated in every division of the plan.

The *shock* quarter saw many changes in important administrative posts, a general campaign for hardening the discipline of labor, and a searching reexamination of the Five-Year Plan from top to bottom for the purpose of discovering weak spots and the most critical elements in the program. In a word, the country was placed on a war basis more than ever before. Strong men were appointed to the more strategic positions in the economic system and persons who failed to get results were ruthlessly shelved or demoted. As a consequence of these changes many of the weaknesses of the preceding quarter were eliminated. However, while the figures for the original plan were generally exceeded, the revised figures for the quarter were for the most part not fulfilled. Only in the case of oil production was the program practically achieved. The most pronounced weaknesses were in the realms of coal, pig iron, machine construction, and transportation of freight.

The year 1931 has been marked by much less excitement than the previous year. The Russian people have settled down to a grim struggle for the fulfilment of the plan in four years. While the totals for the first half of the year are not yet available, certain events of considerable importance have been recorded. The Five-Year Plan for the production of oil was completed early in April. It has also been completed for the area of land under cultivation. But perhaps the largest and most far-reaching achievement of the period was the collectivization of 52.7 per cent of all peasant households on June 1. This would seem to mean that the battle over the land has been won by the revolutionary forces. Numerous factories completed their five-year plans in two and one-half years; and 183 new plants began operations during the first six months of 1931. The Soviet economists, moreover, claim that they have passed England in the smelting of iron ore, and have attained second place to America in oil production and the output of agricultural machinery. This year also witnessed certain shifts of emphasis. Attention was turned toward the improvement of food and housing conditions, the development of municipal utilities, and the promotion of the meat industry. In agriculture the emphasis shifted from the battle for grain, which had been won, to the battle for meat and animal products.

On the other hand, there were, as the Russians say, certain narrow places in the program. The basic industries of coal, iron, and transportation gave trouble, not because they were lagging behind the figures of the Five-Year Plan, but because they were not keeping abreast of the needs of the rapidly growing country. Yet more disturbing were the failures in the realm of management and labor organization. Here undoubtedly is the most vulnerable spot in the entire Soviet program. Strong measures, however, are being taken to work a remedy. In January a credit reform was initiated which sought to place definite financial responsibility on the management of each enterprise. And, on June 23, 1931, Stalin made a speech before a conference of industrial managers which may prove as significant for industry as his famous letter to the press on March 2, 1930, was for agriculture. In this speech he called for the more efficient organization of labor, the rapid mechanization of processes, the abandonment of the principle of equality of wages, the rewarding of skill, initiative, and ability, the payment of wages according to results, the fixing of the responsibilities of management, the promotion of workers regardless of party membership, the moderation of the class struggle in the field of industry, the adoption of a policy of reconciliation toward the members of the old intelligentsia, and the introduction into every enterprise of strict methods of accounting. It was a most realistic and businesslike performance which could hardly be matched among the statesmen of the world. The speech, however, should be regarded in no sense as a surrender to capitalism. The Communists continue to hold all strategic positions in the social order.

This last half-year has witnessed yet another event of great importance—the appointment of a committee of fifty-nine persons to formulate the second five-year plan to cover the years from 1933 to 1937. Its major outlines, which have already been tentatively drawn, indicate that the intensive program of industrialization will continue but that the immediate needs of the population will receive far more attention than in the first five-year plan. According to Kuibyshev, Chairman of the State Planning Commission, "the year 1931 will go down in history as a year of the completion of the foundations of socialist economy in the U.S.S.R. The last year of the second five-year plan, 1937, must and will mark the completion of the building of socialism."

There remain two questions which should be of great interest to us: first, Will the first five-year plan succeed? And second, If it does succeed, how will it affect the rest of the world?

Except for one element in the situation, the answer to the first question would have to be an emphatic affirmative. Everything seems to be going well except one thing. That one thing is management. The Soviet leaders have not been able to live up to their program in raising the efficiency of labor and reducing the costs of production. These failures might prove disastrous. On the other hand, the Communists are well aware of the gravity of the question, as we have seen, and are taking heroic and realistic measures to grapple with it. In view of their past performances in the face of critical situations one may expect that they will deal with this one passably well. I am consequently of the opinion that the Five-Year Plan will have to be regarded as a success, and, in view of the difficulties attending its execution, a brilliant and heroic success.

The bearing of Soviet success on the rest of the world is, of course, a highly speculative matter. The one point here on which all competent observers would probably agree is that it will put the American Government in its policy toward the Soviet Union in a yet more untenable, embarrassing, and even ridiculous position. On the economic side I can see no cause for alarm at Soviet success. In fact there probably should be more cause for alarm if she does not succeed. The prices which she is willing to accept for the goods which she exports will depend very largely on the acuteness of her need. She exports in order to pay for imports which her economy requires. Consequently, in the degree that her need moderates she will be less willing to throw her goods on the world market. The trade between Soviet Russia and the rest of the world would then appear more normal in character. Moreover, as so many observers have pointed out, the Soviet domestic market will remain practically insatiable for many years to come. To be sure, numerous causes of friction between the socialistic and capitalistic systems will continue to arise. And they can be resolved only as the representatives of both systems are prepared to make concessions and to create those conditions which make some measure of understanding possible. One of the most significant results of the success of the Five-Year Plan may well be that it will force the capitalistic countries to recognize the Soviet Union as a permanent addition to the family of nations.

II

To attempt to evaluate any phase of the Soviet experiment today is, of course, a very presumptuous and foolhardy thing to do. Even the best informed among us can have only the most fragmentary knowledge of what is happening in the "first workers' republic of history." And when it comes to gauging the potential strength of the forces at work in a situation so complex, the guess of the stupid may well prove to be as trustworthy as that of the wise. We know of a certainty that certain factors will wax and become more powerful and that others will wane and disappear; but we are never able to determine beyond a reasonable doubt into which category a particular factor will be thrust by the onward sweep of events. Even the most rash of prophets must admit that, when the final reckoning is made, life may show that certain forces which he thought would be decisive left scarcely a trace upon the record, and that others which he failed to observe altogether actually shaped the course of things. Ideas are among the most dynamic elements in human culture; and the Russian revolution has released ideas, as have few of the social convulsions of history. Perhaps some of those ideas, when grown to full stature, will prove to be great ideas; perhaps the revolutionary movement contains the seeds of changes which will affect institutions throughout the world and send reverberations of increasing volume down the corridors of the centuries. It has happened before; it may happen again.

Moreover, in passing judgment on the Soviet experiment the observer from capitalistic countries must always remember that his education from the day of his birth has unfitted him even to understand that experiment. He is literally a bundle of contrary habits, attitudes, ideas, and dispositions. His whole system of values and cast of mind make of him a strongly biased witness. Even when he strives to be entirely objective he may be merely clearing the field so that his deepest and most completely hidden prejudices will be given untrammeled play. The more vital and significant elements of any culture can probably never be sensed until the observer has reached the point of sympathy and understanding which enables him to see that culture from the inside and to look out upon the rest of the world through the medium of its values. The most uncritical travelers to Soviet Russia, by the way, are not those tough-minded persons who visit the country with the firm resolve not to be bamboozled. All too often such persons never actually enter the Union. Psychologically they remain in their own culture and are in much the same position as the first Christians who traveled among the pagans. Although they may seem to visit Moscow, they actually stay at home. They go equipped with a neat package of stereotypes inherited from their ancestors and unwittingly measure everything by standards derived from their own society. The ideological gap which divides the ardent Russian communist from the ordinary citizen of the West is already a huge one. And that gap divides the world into two hemispheres.

Then, too, in passing judgment on the Soviet experiment one must remember that "Rome was not built in a day." Most of the current commentaries on conditions in Russia seem to me to violate this altogether obvious principle. They seem to be based on the assumption that the Bolshevik revolution should be appraised as easily and as quickly as a change in the method of electing the county sheriff. They demand that the revolution prove itself in a few years and that it be conducted according to the very latest rules of parlor etiquette. This, of course, is ridiculous. The revolution called for and has set in motion a program for the radical reconstruction of an entire society. To expect the passions aroused by such a social upheaval to subside in less than a generation would seem to be folly. And the full significance of the ideas which it generated can scarcely be fully realized in less than a century. My suggestion is merely that this thing should be viewed, in so far as it is humanly possible, in proper perspective.

However, in spite of all the difficulties, I shall make at least a gesture in the direction of an appraisal of the Soviet program. At any rate I shall point out those elements in the situation which in my judgment should be taken into account. I shall even engage in some speculations with respect to the future, my only defense for doing this being that it is interesting and that everybody else is doing it. Needless to say, I do not place much confidence in what I have to say, although my tone may at times suggest otherwise.

I shall divide my comments into four parts. In the first I shall point to some of the more important uncertainties in the situation; in the second I shall consider the liabilities of the Soviet program; in the third I shall outline its assets; and in the fourth I shall examine certain of the more common criticisms which have been called forth by the effort to plan the economy.

There are various uncertain quantities in the situation which may greatly influence, if they do not practically determine, the success of the Five-Year Plan and the more general program of the revolutionary forces. Take, for example, the uncertainty regarding the behavior of the elements. Until adequate reserves can be built up, a condition which as yet has not been achieved, a general and continued failure of crops due to drought or pests might well prove disastrous. Soviet Russia is still 80 per cent rural and must for many years to come, therefore, place large dependence on agricultural produce. To-day, because of the effort being made to industrialize the country, such dependence is peculiarly marked. Great quantities of machinery must be purchased from abroad, and in the absence of extensive foreign credits the Government will have to place large reliance on the export of farm products. The enormous extent of the country, however, and the rapid development of new areas would seem to reduce the danger from this direction.

Equally disastrous would be a foreign war, even a war of the most modest dimensions. It would mean the mobilization on a fairly large scale of both man-power and economic resources for non-productive purposes. Since there is practically no surplus of goods in the Soviet Union today, such a mobilization could be achieved only at the expense of definitely sacrificing the program of construction. Certainly, the surest possible guaranty of the peaceful intentions of the Soviet Government at the present juncture is the fact that war would mean the literal scrapping of the Five-Year Plan. The Communist leaders are consequently entirely in earnest when they show alarm at the appearance of even relatively inconspicuous war clouds above the international horizon. Until their heavy industries are well established they will go to almost any lengths to keep the peace. Thereafter, of course, it may be a different story.

A third factor which might seriously affect Soviet success in the immediate future is the world economic situation. The present program of construction postulates the temporary stabilization of capitalism. More than that, its progress is dependent to a considerable degree on the products of capitalistic industry, as well as on the service of capitalistic technology and technicians. The current economic depression in Europe and America, while fanning the fires of unrest and presumably creating conditions favorable to revolution, has been a cause of real anxiety in Soviet councils. It has greatly lowered the value of Soviet goods on the world markets and hampered their program of construction. Thus, although the volume of Soviet exports increased by 57 per cent during the first nine months of 1929–30, their money value increased only 17 per cent. It has been estimated that the Soviet Union lost about 30 per cent on the prices of its products, while it gained only about 15 per cent through price reductions on its imports. A Communist revolution in Germany today, because of the disorganizing effect it would have on German industry for the moment, might well be unwelcome in those circles in Moscow which are supremely devoted to the achievement of the Five-Year Plan.

Another uncertainty which always looms as a possibility is a split within the Communist party. While there is no reason for believing that such an event is in the offing, rule by dictatorship always faces the danger of rapid and catastrophic dissolution. If the Party were to split evenly over some vital issue, the outcome would be almost inevitably the end of the present government. With the passing of the Party, the author and champion of the Five-Year Plan would relinquish its hold on the rudder of the ship of state. To be sure, the fact that the realities of the situation are universally recognized greatly reduces the possibility that the division will occur. The Communists know that they must in some way compose their differences or accept the alternative of abdication, arrest, imprisonment, and the firing squad. Such knowledge is a powerful deterrent to hasty action. Moreover, every success recorded in the realization of the program of construction tends to increase the solidarity of the Party under its present leadership and to improve its standing in the country.

The greatest unknown quantity in the equation probably has to do with human nature. For a hundred and fifty years our economists have told us with a high degree of consistency that the only sound basis for the development of industry is private enterprise and that the driving force back of private enterprise must be material gain. Soviet economists are striving to build on a radically different foundation. They maintain, moreover, that their adversaries misread human nature and that man, if properly nurtured, will labor quite as strenuously and dependably for social as for private ends. Or at least they argue that the rewards for which society's most gifted members strive need not be material in character. Indeed, they carry the battle vigorously into the enemy's camp and contend that for various reasons collectivism will liberate the energies of the masses far more effectively than capitalism. Moreover, the Soviet psychologists are finding that the egoistic impulses of children are somewhat weaker in Russia than they are reported to be in the United States. Also, throughout the length and breadth of their vast educational system the Communists are seeking to mold human nature according to the collectivistic ideal. Whether they will succeed or not is a question which must be left to the future.

Among the distinct liabilities which the Soviet experiment is compelled to carry is the low cultural level of the country. At the time of the revolution probably 70 per cent of the adult population were illiterate. As a consequence the present effort to mobilize the resources of the Union is faced with almost insuperable obstacles. When the whole economy is being expanded at an unprecedented rate, enormous amounts of energy must be devoted to the teaching of millions of grown men and women to read and write and manipulate simple number combinations. These great masses of Soviet citizens will also have to be taught the rudiments of hygiene, science, and politics. The raising of the cultural accomplishments of the population is in itself a stupendous undertaking. When it is linked with a vast program of economic construction, one is justified in wondering whether the success of both undertakings may not be placed in jeopardy. And yet it may well be, as the Bolsheviks have always argued, that the only pedagogically sound method of improving the cultural qualifications of the masses is to place upon them large responsibilities of social reconstruction.

Closely joined with the extreme cultural backwardness is the low level of technical skill and knowledge among the population. With a truly pitiful equipment in comparison with the great industrial sections of the West, the Soviet Union sets itself the task of developing the entire economy at a rate which the most advanced countries would never hope to achieve. At the time of the launching of the Five-Year Plan in 1928 only 41.3 per cent of the workers in Soviet industry were skilled, whereas in Germany the corresponding percentage was 62.6. In the case of engineers the situation was even less satisfactory. For industry as a whole the percentage of engineers to the entire number of workers was .37 in the Soviet Union and 1.38 in Germany. Thus, a people living by means of a primitive agriculture and with almost no general acquaintance with even the simplest types of machinery is seeking to enter completely into the machine age in two or three decades. This fact alone is almost sufficient to explain the failure of Soviet industry to lower the costs of production, raise the efficiency of labor, and improve the quality of goods in accordance with the provisions of the Five-Year Plan. Such achievements can scarcely be reached by any form of political *tour de force,* but must rather wait upon the slow processes of education and the rearing of a new generation bred in the traditions of industrial civilization.

For the most part the revolutionary leaders, at the time they took over the reins of government, lacked that special training in the technical professions which the building of the new society requires. They were extremely proficient in conducting the fight against the Tsar from the prisons and the garrets and the cellars of the world, but they knew little about the building of factories, the construction of railroads, the refinement of metals, and the science of management. Moreover, even the infant industry that developed in the days of the empire was managed very largely by foreigners. All of these things the Communists have therefore had to learn, and they have been going to school to the capitalistic countries on a large scale. They are sending their representatives by the hundred all over the earth for the purpose of learning the secrets of modern industry and agriculture; and they are bringing even larger numbers of foreign technicians to the Soviet Union, there to give of their knowledge and experience in pushing the program forward.

Another distinct liability is a certain tradition of inefficiency which seems to pervade the entire economic structure. This is no doubt traceable in part to factors already mentioned—the low cultural level, the inadequacy of the technical staff, and the relative lack of managerial talent. Also an unintelligent bureaucracy, the expected accompaniment of socialism, has reached out its long tentacles to strangle initiative and needlessly to complicate the conduct of business. Almost nothing in the Soviet Union is done quickly and with dispatch. Transactions which should require minutes take hours, and transactions which should be handled in hours may consume whole days. As a consequence, one of the most common forms of occupation is simple waiting. The Russian people apparently have never developed a sense of the value of time. This may be an admirable trait in many respects, but it is more suited to an agrarian than to an industrial civilization. The

Party is of course keenly alive to the importance of this whole question and is carrying on a continuous campaign by all the means at its disposal to eliminate the evils of bureaucracy and to raise the efficiency of administration. Stalin's famous speech on June 23, 1931, before a conference of industrial managers, represents the culmination of a series of measures taken to raise the efficiency of labor and fix responsibility in the management of industry.

The situation is greatly aggravated by the spirit of class struggle which touches practically every phase of life and which was made more acute at many points by the launching of the great plan. The manifestations of this spirit are partly the fruit of Marxian doctrines, partly a heritage of the revolt of the intelligentsia during the first years of the revolution, and partly the product of a genuine conflict which still continues at home and abroad between the Soviet Government and the surviving remnants of the former ruling groups—monarchists, landlords, capitalists, and aristocrats. The entire economic and social structure is permeated by an element of suspicion and distrust. On the side of the Communists there is a deep-seated fear lest highly placed members of the technical and managerial staff resort to the sabotage of the program of construction. And while they have probably exaggerated and made political capital out of every attempt at counter-revolution, widespread plots to wreck the plans of the new government undoubtedly have been uncovered. The severity and ruthlessness with which these conspiracies have been put down, combined with the precariousness of the position occupied by all members of the old intellectual classes, have

tended to paralyze the will of numbers of technicians and engineers who were identified in some way
with the former *régime*. Feeling themselves dis-
trusted by their proletarian masters, they are unable to give the full measure of devotion to their
work and probably in many instances secretly cherish the overthrow of Soviet rule. Until a new intellectual class has been produced by the revolution
(one of the major aims of the system of higher education), this condition is likely to continue and to
constitute one of the most powerful obstacles to
success. In the meantime, every member of the old
intelligentsia is regarded as guilty until by his
works he proves himself innocent beyond any possibility of doubt. However, that this period of conflict
is drawing to a close is also suggested by the speech
of Stalin already referred to. In this speech he certainly holds out the olive branch to this suspected
class.

Another important liability is the attitude of the
capitalistic nations and particularly of the United
States toward the Bolshevik program. At any rate
the burdens of the Soviet Government have not
been lightened by the expressions of ill will which it
has encountered throughout the world. This situation no doubt is due in part to historical causes, but
it must be traceable in large measure to the challenge which the revolutionary movement throws out
to capitalistic society. Also, in various ways the
Communists have apparently endeavored to embarrass and irritate the ruling groups in other countries. In this endeavor they have usually succeeded
admirably. Thus, the antireligious campaign, though
generally misrepresented in the American press,

must have postponed considerably the day when official relations will be established between the Soviet Union and the United States. Then, too, no matter what the facts may be, the Soviet Government is always regarded as wholly responsible for the actions of the Third International in every corner of the globe. Indeed, our politicians have even sought to blame Moscow for the economic depression, the fall of the price of wheat, and almost anything else which they have difficulty in explaining to their constituents. But whatever the cause of the hostility of foreign nations, it is a genuine factor in determining the success of the Five-Year Plan. If large credits could be secured in the money markets of the world, and particularly in the money markets of America, the whole program of construction would go forward much more rapidly and easily. Its effects on international trade also would be much more normal in character.

A final liability which must be reckoned with is the individualistic tradition of the peasant. While this tradition is much less extreme than among the farmers of America, where each family lives on its own land and looks with a trace of suspicion at the nearest neighbor half a mile away, it is nevertheless a real factor in the situation. Whether the victory of the Soviet Government over this tradition will prove as easy as it seems today remains to be seen. That the peasant can be made to change not only his way of life but also his outlook upon the world in such a brief period would appear to be highly doubtful. And yet few competent observers are ready to defend the thesis that the peasant will ultimately return to his small strip of land.

Placed high among the assets favoring the success of the Soviet experiment is a certain courage or daring on the part of the leadership. Lenin was undoubtedly one of the greatest political figures of history. And for steadfastness, courage, integrity, realism, and ability to extract the essence from a situation, it would be very difficult to match Stalin among the statesmen of the West. Under the Communist leadership the slate has been wiped as clean as could be for the charting of the new order. A premium, consequently, has been placed on bold social invention, and creative energy has been released on a scale seldom witnessed in the past. Although many of the innovations introduced by the Communists will, of course, prove sterile, certain of them should be fruitful and serve to demolish powerful barriers to social advance which in other societies, because of inertia or vested interest, effectually block the way. To be sure, the tendency toward the wholesale rejection of practices linked with pre-revolutionary times, on the ground that they are *bourgeois,* and the too narrow concentration on the cult of the proletariat no doubt will result on occasion in throwing away the good with the bad and in sedulously nursing spurious values. Yet it must be confessed that Soviet leaders have been very ready to borrow ideas from capitalistic society.

If Soviet Russia were the size of Hungary, daring in leadership would be of little avail—as history clearly proves. An experiment so bold must be defended by great spaces and must possess enormous natural resources. The Soviet Union has both in abundance. It occupies almost one-sixth of the land surface of the globe and is two and one-half times the size of continental United States. During the period of civil war and intervention this vast area was an invaluable and even indispensable asset. Indeed, if the country had been small in extent, the revolutionary order almost certainly would have been snuffed out within a few months. Then the Union possesses large reserves of almost all of the more important natural resources. While its supply of coal is far less than that of the United States, it is sufficient for many generations. In the spheres of soil, timber, peat, oil, and certain metals, the Union occupies an unrivaled position. The varied climate makes possible the raising of anything from parrots to polar bears and from cotton to icebergs. If ever a country were equipped by nature to carry on a great social experiment, that country is the Soviet Union. As soon as its heavy industries are established, it will be able, if need be, to carry on an independent existence. Within its own borders may be found practically all of the natural products upon which civilization rests.

Inhabiting this wide territory are 182 different races and peoples. Although many of these racial and national groups are small and without highly developed cultures, the great body of the population of the Union comes from Slavic stock. The potentialities of any people cannot of course be foreseen; but enough is already known of the Russian Slav to make prophecy unnecessary. The race has shown all of the abilities which are needful in building a great industrial civilization, unless it be ability in the field of administration. This ability, however, will no doubt appear as situations arise which call it forth. Certainly, in the great artists and writers of the past century the Russians have shown themselves capable of producing the very first rank of genius. This people, moreover, is unspoiled by civilization: its great creative period lies in the future; obviously it possesses a virility and an inventiveness which certain of the older races seem for the moment to have lost. It probably contains the largest reservoir of talent remaining to be developed among the light-skinned races. Moreover, the variety of stocks and cultures within the Union, combined with the liberal policy of the government toward these minority groups, should result in great cultural fertility. The building of the new society would therefore seem to be in good hands.

Then there are the virtues of planning itself which the Soviet leaders regard as perhaps their greatest asset. Through the State Planning Commission they are able to bring their best intelligence to bear upon the problem of the organization and development of their resources. Under this system, so they argue, there will be none of the great wastes of capitalism. Natural riches will be exploited in the light of the abiding interests of all, and not for the purpose of enriching the few by hurried and wasteful methods of production. The discovery of knowledge in the field of industry will proceed according to a general plan designed to benefit the whole of society, and not in response to the competitive efforts of separate firms, each bent on guarding as precious trade secrets whatever it may learn. Also, according to the Soviet economists, there will be no suppression of invention which purposes to guard private profits at the expense of the general welfare; no industrial crises which periodically shake the economic order

and throw millions of workers out of employment;
no costly advertising which increases the number of
unproductive occupations and drives vast numbers
of persons to live beyond their means; no idle capital which is a useless burden for society to carry and
which is the product of general economic incoördination; no technological unemployment which places
the costs of progress on the shoulders of men and
women least fit to bear them; no speculation on the
stock exchange which consumes credit, takes able
men out of production, generates a get-rich-quick
psychology among the people and contributes to the
development of the tradition that "only saps
work"; no struggles for world markets which turn
nation against nation, breed economic rivalries and
military conflicts, and threaten to destroy civilization in the holocaust of war. This is of course an
extremely optimistic view, but the possibilities resi-
dent in the union of bold social planning with modern technology remain to be demonstrated.

A closely related question of very great significance is the Soviet attempt to organize and plan the
work of science. The entire area of science is being
carefully worked over and the appropriate research
programs and institutes are being outlined and
planned. As a consequence the attack upon both near
and remote problems relating to the life of the country will be no longer left to chance. That institu-
tional autonomy which characterizes the work of
science in our own country is completely rejected.
Even the individual scientist is supposed to engage
in research which fits into the general plan. However, in spite of reports to the contrary, there is no
disposition on the part of the Communist leaders to

concentrate effort on the narrowly and immediately practical. They are convinced that their inclusive and coördinated promotion of research will give their society great advantages in the competition with capitalism.

Another element of great strength in their system, so they believe, is the development of an increasingly intimate relationship between education and social planning. On the one hand, the major instrument for the achievement of any program of construction is a vast educational system which embraces not only the schools but also practically all of the formative and cultural agencies of society. On the other hand, the existence of a definite social program has a profound influence on the processes and purposes of education. The Soviet school is more closely related to life than any other school in the world. Both teachers and pupils participate actively in socially useful labor, in the building of the new order. And at the higher levels the school is assigned definite tasks of vocational and professional training that cannot be evaded. The programs of these institutions are derived directly from the calculated occupational needs of the country during the years immediately ahead. This relating of the school to society makes of education neither a luxury nor a frivolity, but a necessary and serious function of the community.

Another possible asset which the Communists enjoy is the relative simplicity of the economy which they inherited from the Tsar. Their efforts at planning could therefore begin on a small scale and under relatively manageable conditions. As the economic order expands and grows and absorbs modern

technology, their planning organs and processes
may be expected to keep pace. Bit by bit a vast and
complicated system will evolve for planning and
controlling a modern industrial economy. For us to
introduce a system of economic planning into our
society would seem to be a much more difficult undertaking. The system may already be complex beyond human understanding and powerful vested interests bar the way to economic coördination. Moreover, because of the ability of an incoördinated,
primitive agrarian order to take punishment, the
Soviet leaders could fumble about for a number of
years without inviting complete disaster. In our
case much less fumbling can be permitted.

The Communists also contend that one of their
greatest assets is the superiority of the moral foundations of the order which they are endeavoring to
build. All of the organized forces of society are
wrestling directly and unequivocally with the central
problems of the masses. Take the case of the Five-
Year Plan as an example. If every project outlined
there should be achieved, not a single man would
pile up a great private fortune, unless he should do
so by some form of corruption. Then, if he were discovered, as he probably would be, unless he buried
his treasure in the ground or transported it to some
foreign country, he would be arrested, tried, and
punished. The point to be emphasized is that the
central object of the vast program of construction
under way is not to enrich the few but rather to improve the conditions of life of the many. A great
nation is organizing to abolish poverty, to solve the
problem of unemployment, and to abolish the pau-
perism of sickness and old age; to reduce the length

of the working day, to raise the standard of living, and to place medical facilities at the disposal of all; to wipe out illiteracy and superstition, to make educational opportunities universal, and to bring art and science into the service of the masses. Under these conditions an honest appeal can be made to the people to bend their energies to the achievement of the program. They can be asked with a clear conscience to sacrifice, and then to sacrifice again. It is a vision of unquestioned power and appeal.

All of these factors working together have already produced a degree of earnestness and spiritual fervor among those elements committed to the revolutionary program that can be matched only in the more profound religious movements of history. The Communists and their followers in the general population are thoroughly convinced that they speak not only for themselves but also for the great masses of men everywhere and even for the generations yet to come. The critic may say that they are mistaken in their faith, but he can scarcely question their honesty or integrity. To be sure, there are in Soviet Russia today millions who are indifferent and yet other millions perhaps who are embittered; but those who are imbued with the revolutionary tradition are confident that their ideas will conquer the world. In the severe trials of the present they are upheld by the unfaltering conviction that time itself fights in their ranks, and that by some happy stroke of fortune they have become the instruments of mankind's greatest struggle for freedom. Whether they are right or wrong, this faith adds greatly to their strength.

In conclusion I wish to examine four criticisms

which are commonly made of the Soviet program:
first, that the Communists will be unable to manage
the great plants which are being built under the direction of foreign technicians; second, that they are
merely striving now to get what we already have,
namely, material abundance; third, that they are
committed to the worship of the machine; and
fourth, that social planning necessarily results in a
denial of personal freedom and the general regimentation of life.

The contention that the Communists will be unable to administer efficiently the great plants which
are being built under the direction of foreign technicians has, I think, been satisfactorily disposed of
by Dean Donham of Harvard. He has written as follows: "Of course Russia has a big job on her hands
to train her labor to use machinery. I doubt, however, if her task is half as difficult as our task of
training our business men to work coöperatively in
carrying out a general plan." (Or, he should have
added, getting these business men to think and act
in terms of the general good of the masses of the
American people.) The statement about the inability
of the Russians to manage the new plants also con-
veys the impression either that there are no Russian technicians outside prison walls or that for
some reason they are taking no part in the present
program of construction. As a matter of fact the
great majority of technicians and engineers in Soviet Russia today are native to the country. There
is also a suggestion here that the Russian nature is
gravely deficient in some respects and that the Soviet citizen can never become efficient in a practical
way. This of course is rank nonsense. The Soviet

difficulties in conducting a modern industrial system are and will be enormous; but they can easily be accounted for in terms of cultural factors which in time, and probably in a very short time as these things go, will disappear. In other words, the inhabitants of the Soviet Union are capable of learning anything that the rest of the human race has been able to learn.

Superficially there may be something in the view that the Communists are getting excited over doing something that we have already learned to do. But fundamentally this view is unsound. There is the tacit assumption here that we have solved the economic question and that we are now looking for new worlds to conquer. The merest glance about us today shows that we have done nothing of the sort. We have, it is true, entered a world of possible plenty. Our achievements in the sphere of production are nothing short of miraculous; we possess the power to produce all of the goods and services that our people could use. But we have not yet devised a system of social arrangements which makes possible the utilization of this power. In a word, the problem of distribution remains unsolved. Now the Communists are endeavoring to borrow our technology, but they also intend to put it to a better social use than we do. Moreover, they are giving much thought, even in the present very difficult period, to the question of what they are to do with the vast economic system which they are now busily engaged in constructing.

The accusation that the Russians are worshiping the machine also contains an element of truth. They talk about machines, they read about machines, they draw pictures of machines, and they go into ecstasies at the sight of a new machine. They study machines in their schools, they write plays in which the machine is the hero, and they dream of inventing machines. All of this, however, merely means that they see in the machine the road to the conquest of the forces of nature and the instrument of the triumph of man in his old, old struggle with the elements. There is in this attitude something of worship, but it is essentially the same as the attitude which men have normally sustained toward the source of their livelihood, whether it be forest, or soil, or sea. Certainly the Communists do not intend to be driven by the machine, as we so commonly are. On the contrary they are seeking to make it obey the human will.

Finally, the Soviet experience does suggest the conclusion that a planned economy involves a denial of personal freedom and the general regimentation of life. The drive for the achievement of the Five-Year Plan certainly overrides the desires and comforts of the individual, or rather we should say that the first five-year plan does. On the other hand, that the fifth such plan will assume this form seems to me to be highly doubtful. The present plan is a product of harsh conditions and requires harsh measures. The individual is called upon to make great sacrifices. But as the struggle for increased production moderates, as it will if the Soviet system works at all, the tension of life will begin to relax, a feeling of security will appear, and the regimentation of the individual will become unnecessary to the guarding of the social interest. Also the point should be made that a five-year plan for America would be very unlike the Soviet plan. Our industrial plant has been constructed. The need for sacrifice, like that demanded in Russia, simply would not exist. Our problem would be one of utilizing the facilities which we already possess and of distributing economic goods to the population.

This question of freedom should be examined from yet another angle. The Soviet leaders argue that we have less freedom than we think. Moreover, according to their view of things, if there is to be genuine freedom in industrial society, except for the plutocracy, it will come as a result of the planning and the general coördination of life. In other words, the mere assertion of freedom will not bring it into being; nor is the freedom to amass private riches in natural resources and the tools of production the most important form of freedom. In the pre-industrial era, to be sure, when life was simple and the small family group was practically self-sufficient, freedom was essentially a matter of the protection of property and the abolition of external restraints imposed by bandits, despots, and distant governments. But today, because of the growth of the corporate life, liberty is no longer a natural state to be preserved by negation: it must be created and maintained by collective action. This means that men must combine increasingly not only to preserve order, but also to perform the ordinary social functions. At least, society as a whole must accept sooner or later the responsibility for satisfying the basic economic needs of the population and of establishing a condition of general material security for all. In a world where great masses of people live in poverty and the grim specters of sickness, unemployment, and old age perpetually hover in the background, there can be no real freedom. These evils can be laid to rest in industrial society only through organization and by placing definite limitations on the exercise of certain forms of freedom characteristic of historic capitalism. At least so say the Soviet leaders through their system of planning organs and the first five-year plan.

THE ECONOMICS OF FASCISM

BY LUIGI VILLARI

THE ECONOMICS OF FASCISM

I. Origins of the Corporative System

THE general economic situation of Italy is fairly well known to that part of the American public which follows international affairs.

I shall, therefore, limit myself to those aspects of the subject which are more closely associated with Fascism, where Fascist economic policy differs from that of other systems.

In particular I shall deal with the corporative system, which goes far beyond the mere trade-union organization and has expanded into a form of general economic planning affecting every branch of national production.

In this first lecture I shall describe the origins of the present Italian economic system. In the next I shall deal in greater detail with the syndicates, collective contracts, justice in labor disputes, etc. In conclusion I shall sketch out the main results obtained and certain special features of state activity in economic matters.

The States of medieval Italy, especially the city republics, with their great commercial and industrial development, had evolved an elaborate system of corporations or guilds, but although these bodies played an important part in the economic and political history of the times, I need not enter into a detailed account of them, which would be outside the scope of this lecture, inasmuch as the circumstances in which they arose are so different from those of today that the analogies to be derived from them, although historically important, are apt to be misleading. Similar institutions existed in other countries.

The chief interest of these guilds for us lies in the fact that they prove the natural tendency of all communities with a highly developed economy to work out some form of the guild system.

In the eighteenth century, with its intensified individualism, the guilds found many opponents, and in 1776 the French Minister Turgot issued a decree abolishing the *"maîtrises et jurandes"* as incompatible with the new spirit of the age, and although six months later he restored them, and the French Revolutionary Government, by a decree of August 21, 1790, granted to all citizens the right of association without public control in the name of the general principles of liberty, the hostility to the system persisted and indeed became more intense. The fear of strikes, which might be organized by the use or abuse of such forms of liberty to the detriment of the general principles of the Revolution, induced the Government to go back on this concession, and on June 14, 1791, the so-called Le Chapelier law definitely abolished all guilds and corporations and forbade all coalitions or combinations between employers, merchants, workers, or artisans in any trade or profession. This law put an end to the medieval guild system, or such parts of it as still survived in France; other countries subject to the political and cultural influences of the French Revolution followed suit.

The Le Chapelier law constituted the beginning of the general hostility to all forms of working-class solidarity at a time when the industrial revolution was already in operation and the great concentrations of workmen were being formed. This hostility was inspired on the one hand by the fears of the French bourgeois revolutionary *régime* of a rebellion from below, and on the other by the fears of the antirevolutionary but likewise bourgeois *régimes* restored after 1815 lest working-class organizations should lend assistance to the Liberal and Nationalist movements then fermenting in most European countries. In both cases the fears were the outcome of the juridical theories of the French Revolution, which affected even the reactionary governments of the Restoration.

In England, where the danger of an anarchical movement after Waterloo was more real than is generally supposed, severe anti-combination laws were enacted. They were abolished after the labor agitations of the first half of the nineteenth century, and the trade-unions soon assumed a vast development, which at first was essentially non-political and had nothing to do with the Socialist movement, then also beginning to make itself felt.

In France, similar anti-combination laws, in harmony with that of Le Chapelier, continued to exist and were rigidly enforced under the July Monarchy. The Second Republic gave a free hand to the working-class unions, and although with the establishment of the Second Empire the old prohibitions were restored, they were not rigorously enforced, and an increasing toleration was extended to workmen's unions. The right of combination was definitely recognized by the Waldeck-Rousseau law of 1884, which permitted the formation of both workers' and employers' unions, at a time when social legislation throughout Europe only contemplated the former.

In Italy the trade-union system developed later than elsewhere, because industrial life was only in its infancy in the early nineteenth century. Italy has practically no coal, very little iron, and a scarcity of most other raw materials. Hydro-electric power was not developed until the last decades of the nineteenth century. When Italian unity was achieved in 1861 there were very few large businesses, and it was the small artisan class which predominated. There was the old silk industry in Lombardy and some other areas, which was prosperous, but conducted on a comparatively small scale; a few ironworks and mechanical plants existed in different parts of the country, and some textile works in the Neapolitan provinces which were hard hit by the more progressive industries of the north after the unification of the country and the abolition of customs barriers within its borders. Industry as a whole was so unimportant that the first statistical year book of the Kingdom devoted only three pages to it. The total capital invested in limited liability companies in 1864 amounted to barely $270,000,000, and although there was a good deal more capital invested in businesses not organized as limited companies, the total amount was very small. It was natural that the trade-union system should find but little scope in so undeveloped an industrial organism.

Agriculture was a much more important branch of Italian economic life, but it was conducted on patriarchal lines in which any form of trade-unionism was then inconceivable.

The pioneer of labor organization in Italy was Giuseppe Mazzini. The unification of the country, although it represented the realization of his dream, caused him profound disappointment in that it did not assume a republican form, and in his later years he devoted part of his activities to sterile and useless plottings in favor of a republic which nobody outside a small minority wanted. But he also undertook a more practical work in organizing the first unions among the workingmen of Italy to promote not only their material but also their moral and spiritual welfare, and to teach them both their rights and their duties as good citizens. In this propaganda he was inspired by that mystical form of Christianity and that patriotic fervor which characterized his whole spiritual life; but this spirit was at the time above the heads of the majority of the Italian working classes. He soon found himself opposed by the ultra-materialistic teachings of the Marxian International. Karl Marx, who referred to Mazzini as "that eternal old donkey," sent the Russian Bakunin to Italy to undermine Mazzini's position as the leader of Italian democracy and wean the growing labor movement from his influence. Bakunin made use of Mazzini's introductions and support to secure the confidence of the Italian laboring masses, and then proceeded to discredit him in their eyes and to preach a new labor gospel definitely hostile to every form of patriotism, religious belief, or moral duty.

In the end Mazzini was defeated and Marx's theories of pure materialism supplanted his idealism. Mazzini died a broken and disappointed man, and at the point of death his disheartened cry of woe was, "Better the return of the Austrians than the setting up in Italy of those false and perverse doctrines which would divide Italians into oppressors and oppressed."[1]

The "false and perverse doctrines" were destined to prevail in Italy for many years. The trade-union movement developed and expanded to a remarkable degree with the growth of the country's economic life, and especially with the rapid progress of industry. Not only, however, did it play an important part among the industrial communities, but also among the workers on the land, a development which in many other countries has even to this day made comparatively little progress. But unlike the British trade-union movement, that of Italy very soon assumed a political character, and its early strength and subsequent weakness lay in its close association, eventually developing into a regular alliance, with political parties whose object was not solely to improve the conditions of the working masses, but to destroy the whole political system and to coöperate with international movements of a revolutionary character in other lands.[2]

If originally these parties were genuinely inspired by the wish to improve the economic conditions of the Italian workers, which at that time really did need improvement, they had ended by becoming

[1] See *Mazzini e Bakunine,* by Nello Rosselli (Turin: Bocca, 1927).

[2] The alliance between the Italian General Confederation of Labor, which grouped practically the whole organized labor movement, and the Socialist party was denounced after the breakdown of the general strike of August 1, 1922, but the spiritual union of these bodies persisted, until the G. C. L. dissolved itself.

purely political organizations, and neglecting their
social activity. Thus the trade-unions were drawn
into a sphere which was not their own and where
they could do little to promote the welfare of their
members or of the working class in general. The
workers' unions were used as political instruments
to fight against the Government and the institutions
of the country, including the Monarchy and the
Church; but to secure the support of the working
masses the Socialists and other revolutionary groups
had to offer them material advantages in the matter
of wages, labor conditions, and the promotion of social legislation. For the purpose they organized
strikes, often accompanied by violence, to wrest
these advantages from the employers; or if their
own resources were not sufficient, they tried to secure the support of the Government and of the
dominant non-Socialist political groups in the Chamber of Deputies. I say the Chamber advisedly, because it had become the sole source of power.

The employers reacted and formed powerful
unions of their own to defend their interests against
the demands of the workers which were often not
only excessive from a purely economic point of view,
but were also sometimes of a non-economic nature.
The result was a state of latent civil war. Strikes,
sometimes on a large scale, were proclaimed both to
secure higher wages and shorter hours, and to protest against the dismissal of a workman, the promotion of a better man over the heads of others less in-
dustrious, the employment of non-union men, etc.
Disputes arose over the recognition of this or that
union. The employers retorted by proclaiming lockouts, and they too appealed to the Government and

to Parliament. Sometimes one side triumphed, sometimes the other, but the result was always the same —production was held up for a longer or shorter period, and the consumers, including not only the workers and the employers, but the outside public as well, suffered.

The strike movement extended even to the public services—the railways, the post office, the civil service, including the officials of the various departments of the Government. It sometimes happened that a Cabinet Minister, who had refused some concession to his dependents, was greeted with insults in his own Ministry.

There were interminable disputes not only over wages and hours and the other matters referred to above, but over the introduction of labor-saving machinery and the methods for settling labor conflicts. In many cases the strikers were incited by their leaders to violent demonstrations against the employers and the authorities; the police and the troops had to be called out to maintain order, and bloodshed on both sides often occurred. On other occasions strikes were proclaimed out of solidarity with other groups of workmen, and they sometimes developed into general strikes through a whole city or province or even over a wider area.[3] But the result was always the same—the holding up of production to the prejudice of the country as a whole.

[3] These outbreaks and their repression always aroused the most violent manifestations of protest on the part of the Extreme Left, and demonstrations were staged to protest against the reactionary policy of the Government and to express sympathy with the victims. One of the chief benefits of the present *régime* is the complete elimination of these episodes of violence.

As the Government usually gave way to violence, violence was encouraged as the only means of securing the satisfaction of legitimate or illegitimate demands.

The situation feared and deplored by Mazzini was thus to a large extent realized—the division of the Italian people into two hostile classes waging savage warfare against each other. The hatred which the revolutionary leaders succeeded in arousing against the employers and the Government was no less bitter than that which might arise between two nations at war with each other. The social question and class war dominated Italian life and threatened to drain its very lifeblood. Although the workers' unions had a comparatively small membership, they controlled the working class.

The Marxian theory, accepted perhaps more fully in Italy than in any other country, was that of the unity of the proletariat of the whole world against the capitalists of the whole world. But this international solidarity often took the form of waging war against the capitalists of Italy alone, and aimed at securing the support both of the proletariat of other countries and of the governments and governing classes of foreign countries unfriendly to Italy and Italian policy. The leaders denounced every form of patriotism in Italy as the device of the Italian capitalists to crush the Italian workers, and did their best to instil hatred of Italy herself among the Italian masses.

These theories did not, of course, receive universal acceptance or application, and there were periods and areas in which there were no disputes of a violent character in any industry. In agriculture the trouble was limited to the Romagna, where the peasantry were better off than in any other part of Italy, the province of Parma, Apulia, parts of Sicily, and to a few other sections of the country.

Similar troubles occurred, of course, in other countries of Europe and elsewhere, but a poor country like Italy, whose economic life was only beginning to develop, whose production and working capital were still insufficient, could ill afford such disorders. An attempt to realize Mazzini's aspiration to achieve class collaboration was made by Pope Leo XIII with his *Encyclica Rerum Novarum* in 1891. But it led to no practical results.

The Government's attitude was agnostic. It did not pronounce itself for or against either party in the dispute and ignored the labor unions, but it usually ended by extending its support to the strongest of the two parties or to the one which appeared to be the strongest at a particular moment. It was indeed always the strongest, i.e., the party with the greatest resources and the most efficient organization, which won, whatever might be the merits of the dispute.

Then another feature in the economic struggle arose which appeared to be peculiarly Italian—the formation of a multiplicity of unions among the same classes of workers, and this was the outcome of the close connection between politics and the trade-unions. Originally there had been only one type of union which was non-political at first but soon associated with Socialism and even with Communism. In Romagna, where the Republican party had more adherents than elsewhere, including elements of the most diverse nature, Republican unions

were formed and the agrarian struggle was in many
cases largely between the "Red" or Socialist unions
and the "Yellow" or Republican ones. Agricultural
machinery was hired out by the trade-unions to the
farmers and small holders, and there were perpetual
conflicts, often of a violent nature, as to whether the
work was to be performed by a "Red" or "Yellow"
machine. Important Catholic unions were also
formed, organized by the clergy, functioning under
their auspices, and supported by the funds of various Catholic institutions and coöperative societies,
especially in Lombardy and Venetia. There were
also some non-political unions. The multiplicity of
the unions added to the confusion, and made a general settlement of conditions of labor in any trade
difficult, if not impossible. At times the employers
took advantage of this situation to exploit one union
against another.

Early in the twentieth century new tendencies began to appear. A reaction against the predominance
of professors and professional men of the middle
class and also against the purely parliamentary tac-
tics of the leaders arose in the ranks of the Socialist
party. A more thoroughly proletarian movement
was demanded in some quarters to make Italian Socialism more practical and less doctrinaire. Syndicalism, which at first appeared as an extreme form
of Socialism, rebelled against the leaders of the
party. The theory of the general strike was advocated, particularly by Professor Labriola, and in
September, 1904, a general national strike was actually proclaimed for no particular purpose. Among
the Syndicalists Benito Mussolini himself played an
active part, but as the French leader, Sorel, the

founder of Syndicalism, said, Mussolini was no ordinary Socialist.

A more moderate form of Socialism, of which Bissolati and Bonomi were the chief exponents, called itself Reformist and opposed methods of violence. In 1911 it supported the Giolitti Government in its African policy. It became subsequently a regular party, but was dissolved soon after the War.

No less important was the Nationalist movement, which was to meet the Syndicalists halfway and to evolve a new economic theory for the welfare of the whole Italian people without distinction of class, and based on national collaboration. In the first years of the century a Nationalist-Syndicalist group had been formed in Turin advocating the class struggle only within the limits of national solidarity and direct action in the economic field without hostility to the state. Enrico Corradini, who was then beginning to come into prominence as a man of letters and a journalist, advanced the theory of a national struggle combined with a class struggle. If, he declared, there were proletarian classes face to face with the capitalist classes, there were also proletarian nations face to face with the capitalist nations; Italy was a proletarian nation and she must struggle to secure a greater share of the world's wealth now unfairly detained by other states which had taken advantage of her past divisions and weakness to exclude her from colonial territories, the sources of raw materials and world markets. A new generation of Italians must arise to promote the greatness and consequently the wealth of Italy, but for this purpose all classes must collaborate in the struggle for common ends. The Italian proletariat could not achieve a prosperous economic position and a higher moral standing unless the nation as a whole were prosperous and respected.

The Nationalists, although full of enthusiasm and thoroughly sincere in their views, were few in numbers, not backed by wealth or powerful organizations, and appealed more to the intellectual classes than to the working masses or the business world. One of the leading figures of this alliance between Nationalism and Syndicalism was Filippo Corridoni, who saw in this struggle a continuation of the Risorgimento; he believed that only by another revolutionary war could the Italian people achieve their complete independence. He, like Mussolini, had on the very eve of the World War taken an active part in the so-called "Red Week" of June, 1914, which was to emancipate the Italian proletariat both from capitalism and from its unfaithful leaders. As soon as the World War broke out Corridoni became an ardent interventionist. He joined the Garibaldian volunteers who fought in France, and when Italy herself entered the war he returned home, joined the Italian army, and was killed in action. He is regarded today as one of the spiritual fathers of Fascism.

Another man who largely inspired the new movement was Edmondo Rossoni. He had spent many years in the United States as an organizer of the Italian workers in that country, and like other Italians who have lived among their fellow citizens in foreign lands, he had come to realize that the Italian emigrant worker would always be on a footing of inferiority as long as his country was impotent and despised.[4] Rossoni did not believe in the melting-pot theory, for he saw how the differences between various nationalities in the great cities of America persisted, and how the Italian workers remained in a position of inferiority. During the war he returned to Italy and founded the Italian Syndical Committee, which afterward became the Unione Nazionale del Lavoro, a Syndicalist organization of a patriotic character. In the spring of 1919, when Mussolini had founded the first Fascio, Rossoni's organization entered into collaboration with it, and hence arose that dual aspect of the Fascist movement—political and national resistance to the violence of the extremists and internationalists on the one side, and the organization of a labor movement based not on class war but on class collaboration on the other. One of the main objects was to wean the working masses from the antipatriotic activities of Socialism and Communism.

This dual aspect has provided arguments for two sets of opponents—those who regard Fascism as a form of conservative reaction for the defense of capitalism, and those who see in it nothing more than disguised Bolshevism or at least Socialism. These two criticisms are of course mutually destructive, but they are stressed by persons who see only one facet of the movement, or by those who understand Fascism a little better but, being prejudicially hostile to it, now advance one criticism and now an-

---

[4] Other Italians of Socialist convictions were converted to the sense of patriotism after studying the conditions of Italian emigrants abroad. This was notably the case of Enrico Ferri after his visit to the Argentine. He had been a prominent Socialist leader, and at the end of his life became a supporter of Fascism.

other, according to the public which they are addressing.

From the first the Fasci showed in their composition the various aspects of the movement. They comprised ex-service men, and men who were too young to have fought in the war; men of many different professions and political origins, but full of youthful enthusiasm; workingmen and peasants who joined it under the leadership of young students and members of the middle class.

While the Fascist groups were spreading all over Italy, national labor syndicates also arose and secured the support of increasing numbers of workers who were weary of the perpetual revolutionary activity imposed upon them, of the tyranny of the Red leaders, and of the absence of all tangible results except the ever recurring strikes which meant suspension of work and wages in addition to the suspension produced by normal unemployment. The new syndicates set themselves to the task of settling labor disputes, which since the end of the war had become excessively frequent, without strikes or violence, and they often succeeded. They also secured concessions of land on rent or sale contracts on favorable terms. This increased their prestige, and sometimes all the members of a Red union would go over in a body to the National or Fascist syndicate.

The movement was at first accepted by the employers, who saw in it a defense of their own interests against anarchy. But later they began to regard it with suspicion as only a slightly chastened form of Red trade-unionism. The workers hailed it as a new organ for the defense of their interests, without involving a suspension of work and wages. The new labor organizations had arisen and were operating sporadically and without system. It was the soldier-poet, Gabriele D'Annunzio, then in the midst of the Fiume venture, who first conceived the idea of a "Corporative State"; in the constitution which he gave to Fiume he divided the population into ten classes or corporations, according to occupation. The scheme was not put into operation at Fiume it-self, but it found many advocates in Italy and con-tributed to inspire the future Italian corporation organization. Most of the leading Italian National-ists adopted the syndical idea, which was to give Fascism its popular character and affirm the theory of nation-wide collaboration. Many former Social-ists such as the late Michele Bianchi, Angelo Oli-viero Olivetti, Sergio Panunzio, and Paolo Orano were also converted to Fascism and helped to or-ganize the new syndicates.

At the Fascist congress held at Rome in Novem-ber, 1921, under the chairmanship of Mussolini, the corporative idea was embodied in the program then elaborated. The state, the program declared, must be reduced to its essential functions as a political and legal organism, the power of Parliament limited to questions concerning the individual as a citizen and the state as an organ for safeguarding and realizing the supreme interests of the nation, whereas the national technical councils are alone competent to deal with the activities of citizens as producers. Corporations should be encouraged as the expression of national solidarity, as a means for developing production, but they must not submerge the individual by arbitrarily leveling all capacities. We have here the foundations of the corporative system in its essentials, although the idea of two legislative bodies—Parliament and the technical councils—has not been carried out; the idea finds some correspondence in the German Constitution, which provides for an advisory *Wirtschaftsrat,* by the side of the political Parliament. In Germany the system has not proved effective, and in Italy it never materialized, for, as we shall see, Parliament and the executive were to remain the supreme organs of government, while the various syndical and corporative organs are invested only with advisory powers in legislative matters.

In January, 1922, a congress of Fascist syndicates was held at Bologna. The confederation of the Fascist syndical corporations was then created, comprising five national corporations (industrial labor, agricultural labor, commerce, middle and intellectual classes, and seamen). This inclusion of the middle and intellectual classes was a novelty in syndical organization, as heretofore labor was regarded as limited to the workers and more particularly to the manual workers. Now instead we have also a corporation of the middle classes and intellectuals comprised in the general scheme of syndical construction.

This organization, of which the secretary and leading spirit was Rossoni, comprised all types of syndicates, those of employers no less than those of workers. Rossoni thus came to control a vast body of economic forces, and one which tried to expand to even greater proportions and might indeed have ended by comprising the whole body of the productive population, and creating an *imperium in imperio.* This was to lead to certain disagreements even among some of the supporters of Fascism, and eventually to the definite separation of the various confederations as autonomous bodies which could only be grouped together, as we shall see later, under the control of the state.

With the advent of the Fascist Government in October, 1922, the syndical movement assumed a new force, destined to supplant Liberalism in the economic field just as Fascism pure and simple was to do in that of politics. As early as May, 1914, Alfredo Rocco, then a professor of law and a publicist, and today Minister of Justice, had written in the Nationalist paper *L'Idea Nazionale* that to the Nationalists syndicalism appeared a force of economic organization which, if liberated from its Socialist tinge and deprived of the revolutionary and anarchical tendencies which had hitherto characterized it, might prove a useful instrument in the service of the Italian nation. His idea then was that mixed syndicates comprising employers and workers were desirable, and he proposed that the old Italian name of corporation[5] should be given them. He had also at the same time advocated the theory, now generally accepted in Italy, that there are not two classes, as the Socialists assert, but many, which are intermingled and dovetailed into each other, the same individual being often both a landowner and a tenant or a day laborer, the owner of a small business or shop and a manual worker.

At that time syndicates of many kinds still continued to exist side by side. While the Fascist syndicates were developing and expanding, absorbing both the ex-members of the other syndicates and a

---

[5] It was the name applied to the medieval guilds.

certain number of persons who had belonged to none, the older trade-unions, "Red" and "White" (Socialist and Catholic), continued to exist, although their membership was declining. Certain categories of workers, notably those employed in the metallurgical and mechanical industries, still adhered to their old unions, which were of a Socialist character; and the printers' union, which was professedly non-political and had always been well run, continued to flourish. But in other trades the non-Fascist unions gradually lost prestige and importance. Not all the men who dropped out of them joined the new syndicates, because the degeneration of the former into political, revolutionary, and money-extracting organizations had attenuated the glamor of trade-unionism in general, and many had lost faith in it altogether. The fact that the money paid into the coffers of the "Red" and "White" unions had evaporated with no tangible result, even when it was not simply pocketed by the leaders and secretaries, made the workers chary of joining new unions which might go the way of the others.

In the ranks of the employers the older non-Fascist unions survived somewhat longer. Many manufacturers preferred to remain members of them, because, as long as they survived by the side of the new Fascist unions, they were non-political and might comprise all the employers of a particular industry; they were, therefore, regarded as more representative of the general interest. But eventually the older employers' unions ended by being absorbed into the Fascist system, and these, like the workers' syndicates, ceased to be exclusive in the sense of comprising only Fascists and were open to all persons engaged in a particular trade, save to men who were definitely revolutionists. As we shall see later, the law does not even now prevent the formation of non-Fascist[6] unions, but as the latter could not secure recognition and could perform no functions useful to their members, they gradually died out.

Two new tendencies were now arising. On the one hand the syndicates were approaching the condition of the trade-unions of foreign countries, in the sense that there was only one union for every industry or branch of industry; as the syndicates were in a position to secure ever greater advantages for their members, the working masses who were minded to join any union at all tended more and more to join these. On the other hand, the opposition to mixed syndicates, at first advocated in many quarters, was becoming more pronounced, and the idea of creating them was finally abandoned.

In August, 1924, a committee of eighteen members had been appointed by the Government to bring about the transformation of the Constitution of the state, and it devoted particular attention to the relations between the state and the syndicates, the reform of the syndicates themselves and their legal recognition, and the preparation of laws for regulating labor conditions and collective contracts and settling labor disputes.

On this last point Fascism had already achieved a notable measure of success. Since the advent to power of the new Government the number of strikes

[6] The syndicates are called Fascist because they are organized under Fascist auspices, but many, if not most, of their members are not necessarily Fascists.

and lockouts had greatly diminished, but they were not definitely outlawed. It was admitted that in certain circumstances such agitations might be legitimate, and indeed some strikes had actually been promoted by the Fascist syndicates themselves, in order to secure for the workers the better conditions to which the Fascist leaders believed them to be legitimately entitled. The progress of the strike movement and its ending are illustrated in the following figures:

Year	Strikes	Strikers	Working Days Lost
1919	1,871	1,554,566	22,213,746
1920	2,070	2,313,685	30,569,218
1921	1,134	725,862	8,110,063
1922	575	422,733	6,916,914
1923	200	66,213	296,462
1924	260	73,013	523,761

The reduction in the number of strikes apparent in 1921 was largely due to the action of the Fascist syndicates in settling labor disputes peaceably. By 1922 the syndicates had acquired still greater authority and importance, as the figures testify. After the advent of the Fascist *régime* the reduction was even more marked. In 1925 strikes fell to negligible figures.

But the final objective aimed at was to eliminate all such forms of violent action altogether. There were rival opinions as to the form the syndicates were to assume, some advocating compulsory membership for all workers of each trade in a single union which was to be a government organ, while others favored absolutely free syndicates wholly independent of government action or control.

The committee of eighteen proposed certain reforms, which I need not enter into as they were afterward considerably modified, concerning labor organization and its representation in the body politic. The employers' organizations raised certain objections to the proposals of the committee, and finally on October 2, 1925, an agreement was arrived at between the employers' General Confederation of Industry and the workers' Fascist General Confederation of Labor (not to be confused with the earlier Socialistic body), known as the Pact of Palazzo Vidoni,[7] under the auspices of Roberto Farinacci, then General Secretary of the Fascist party.

The two Confederations recognized each other as the exclusive representatives of the employers on the one hand and labor on the other, and they agreed that collective labor contracts were to be stipulated between the officially appointed representatives of the dependent syndicates in the two bodies. This agreement was afterward legalized by Royal Decree and thus obtained official recognition and sanction.

With the next phase we have the system as it was finally established and is in force today.

II. The Existing Labor System in Italy

THE existing labor system of Italy is laid down in four enactments—the Law of April 3, 1926, on the juridical regulation of collective labor relations, the Royal Decree of July 1, 1926, for the application of the same law, the Labor Charter of April 21, 1927, and the Law on the Reform of the National Council

[7] Palazzo Vidoni was then and is still the headquarters of the Fascist party.

of Corporations of March 20, 1930. There are other measures concerning particular aspects and details which I need not allude to here.

The Labor Charter is not a law, but a set of principles on which Italian labor legislation is based or should be based in the future, and to which collective labor contracts must conform. Its moral value, as Signor Bottai, Minister of Corporations, said, is equal to that of a law, inasmuch as it is the pronouncement of the Fascist Grand Council, the highest organ of the existing *régime*.

To explain the system thus established it is, I think, better to set forth the main institutions on which it is based, rather than to analyze the various enactments one by one. These institutions are:

    I. Legally recognized syndicates.
    II. Collective labor contracts.
    III. The Labor Courts.
    IV. The corporations.
    V. The Ministry of Corporations.

I. LEGALLY RECOGNIZED SYNDICATES

It should be borne in mind always that Fascism has never been associated with any particular class of the population. The composition of the Fasci from the very first shows that their supporters were recruited from all classes. The syndical policy, like the whole Fascist system, is based primarily on class collaboration. Its founders realized from the beginning that the problems of the organization of production can be settled without national or social disintegration or the abolition or oppression of any class. They also bore in mind that in every aspect of this organization the interests of the consumers, of the nation as a whole, must be considered as well as those of the parties directly concerned. Collaboration and production are its two watchwords, and all people playing an active part in the life of the nation, all those who perform any useful function, whether it be of a material or an intellectual nature, are regarded as producers.

Before the war the Italian trade-unions were associations independent of all public control. The leaders of these unions usually ignored the question of production, and indeed encouraged the workers to work as little as possible, and taught them not to regard badly done work as in any way wrong, since they considered the struggle to be one between the workers, the manual workers in particular, and the capitalists—i.e., those who retain the means of production, a war of the exploited against the exploiters.

Fascism is the contradiction of all this. It is essentially national and has as its first objective the increase of the wealth of the nation as a whole, consequently of all classes, and it aims at grouping all the working population into associations in order to organize them on a professional basis. This grouping is both vertical and horizontal—the syndicates, the federations, and the confederations representing the vertical grouping, and the corporations the horizontal grouping. The former bodies are autonomous, but recognized by the state and under a certain measure of public control. The corporations are state organs, grouping all associations and interests, whether of employers or workers, in a particular branch of economic activity.

The syndicates, although autonomous, are insti-

tutions of public right, i.e., legally recognized bodies
with legal responsibilities and the right to legal action.

For every profession, trade, or occupation in
every district, a syndicate of employers and one of
workers may be formed and may secure legal recognition. Only one syndicate may be recognized for
each category and in each district. To secure recognition the syndicate, if it is of employers, must comprise members employing at least 10 per cent of the
workers in a particular branch of trade in the district concerned; if it is a workers' union its members
must be at least 10 per cent of the workers in the
particular trade and district. One-tenth may seem a
small proportion, but we must remember that in
Italy the trade-union principle was not as widespread as in some other countries, particularly in
Great Britain and Germany. In actual fact most of
the syndicates comprise a far larger proportion of
workers than one-tenth, and many comprise practically the totality of the persons concerned.

Another requisite for legal recognition is that the
syndicate shall have not solely economic and material objects, but also functions of an educational
character: that it should promote the moral, technical, and patriotic education of its members. It
should further provide for social services, sick benefits, etc. It must therefore set aside a part of its
revenues for these purposes. All members must
offer guaranties of capacity, morality, and patriotism. As I said before, it is not necessary for them
to be Fascists. From the political point of view, only
persons notoriously associated with seditious activities are excluded from the syndicates. In practice a

certain number of such persons have gained admission to the syndicates, but if they do not continue to conduct seditious propaganda, they are left undisturbed. Higher qualifications are, of course, required in the executive officers than in the ordinary members. No one need join the legally recognized syndicate of his trade unless he wishes to do so; but as the syndicate represents all the workers or employers of the category concerned and defends the interests of them all, all persons enjoying its protection must pay their contributions, which are the equivalent of one day's wages per annum in the case of the workers;[8] in the case of the employers other criteria are applied to fix the amounts due. The registered members of the syndicate may be called upon to pay some small extra contributions for their membership card and badge. Each syndicate drafts its own regulations and fixes its own method of electing its executive officers.

On February 28, 1931, the employers' syndicates were 680, with a membership of 1,220,551 businesses; the firms represented were in all 4,346,485 (including members and non-members). The workers' syndicates were 3,550, with 3,468,539 members; and about 9,000,000 persons in all were represented by them. The professional syndicates were 1,028, with 92,425 members and 115,000 persons represented. In all 5,258 associations, with about 4,800,000 members, and over 11,000,000 persons represented. The membership is constantly on the increase, but the syndical officers are in no hurry to secure large numbers of members, preferring a certain selection.

[8] This is smaller than the contribution paid to the old labor unions; and many who belonged to the latter failed to pay.

The workers' confederations have a larger membership than the old General Confederation of Labor ever had. Before the war its membership had never reached 400,000, and even in the years of Red domination, 1919–22, it numbered only 2,200,000 members paying their contributions.

As I said before, the recognized syndicate is an autonomous body, but subject to state control, which finds expression in various provisions; thus while the president and secretary are elected according to the statutes of each syndicate, they must receive the approval of the state before they can take up their duties. In cases of grave irregularities the public authority may dissolve the governing body of the syndicate and transfer its powers to the president, the secretary, or an outsider appointed *ad hoc* as special commissioner, and in the most serious cases it may even withdraw recognition. In actual practice there is very little interference on the part of the authorities in the activities of the syndicates, except in cases of flagrant financial irregularity.

Each syndicate must have its own representative organ to act for it in labor disputes and in negotiations with syndicates representing other classes. Mixed committees[9] may be formed for a particular purpose, comprising representatives of workers' and employers' syndicates on an equal basis. The mixed committees fulfilled the functions now to be intrusted to the corporations or the sections of the National Council of Corporations, and they still do so where the corporative system is not yet fully operative.

[9] These are not to be confused with mixed syndicates of employers and workers, which are not permitted.

A syndicate possessing the necessary requisites may apply for recognition, but it need not do so. If it wishes to secure recognition, it must send in an application to the Minister of Corporations, with a detailed account of its origins, activities, a list of its members and officers, and a copy of its regulations. Recognition is granted by Royal Decree on the proposal of the Minister of Corporations.

The chief function of the recognized syndicates is to stipulate collective labor contracts, which they alone are competent to do.

All syndicates are legally responsible for their actions and must set aside a part of their funds for meeting such responsibilities.

The law permits the existence of *de facto* associations without legal recognition, but no individual may belong both to a recognized syndicate and a non-recognized one having the same objects. Private associations may, of course, be formed for non-syndical purposes, but syndicates without legal recognition and powers have no legal status to negotiate contracts or represent their members; they are therefore of no practical value and have gradually disappeared.

Besides the syndicates of employers and workers, there are also intermediate syndicates of technical experts, managers, clerks, farm bailiffs, etc. These represent a new feature in the trade-union system; such categories of workers had hitherto been usually ignored. Technical experts and administrative employees may be grouped in the same syndicate, but they must constitute separate sections with separate representative organs. Managers of works have their own associations.

Artisans working on their own account also have their syndicates grouped under the Autonomous Federation of Artisan Communities; similar associations exist for small traders, commission agents, and small farmers, and to small holders working their own land.

In 1927 the leaders of the socialistic General Confederation of Labor came to the conclusion that under the Fascist syndical system its own postulates would be accepted and applied, and it consequently dissolved itself. Members of the liberal professions —lawyers, doctors, engineers, authors, artists, etc.— are also included in the corporation system; indeed, great importance is attached to the middle classes and to intellectual values in general. These professional men are grouped in local syndicates according to their professions in the district in which they reside.

All these various syndicates are in turn grouped under larger organizations—national syndicates of a particular category of workers, and confederations including all who are employed in a particular branch of trade throughout the country; but the employers and the workers are enrolled in separate organizations. The associations are of various grades. The syndicates of workers or employers in a particular district—a municipality, a province, a larger area—or in some cases the whole country, are associations of the first grade. Those of the second grade are formed by a group of associations of the first, those of the third by a group of the second, and so on.

Not in all trades and professions are all these various groups to be found. The formations vary according to the importance and nature of the particular trade in each area.

The syndicates of the first grade comprise the workers of a particular trade (e.g., printing, metallurgy, building, etc.) in a province or larger area, or, in the case of some special trade, the whole country. If in one province there are many local associations of a particular trade, they are grouped in a single provincial association.

The national federations group all the syndicates of a particular trade throughout the country while the provincial unions and national federations are grouped under the national confederation concerned.

In the case of the employers' associations the first grade is represented by the mixed territorial associations. The various firms are furthermore grouped in national associations of their particular industry. The provincial union is syndical and deals with the stipulations of labor contracts, etc.; the federations are economic bodies whose function is to interpret the needs of the industry as a whole. Thus a firm operating a motor-car plant in Turin is included in the Turin Industrial Union, which comprises all the other industries, of whatever nature, in the province, and also forms part of the national federation of motor-car manufacturers of the whole country.

There are certain local industrial unions limited to a particular area of a province in which industry is widely developed. In areas where industry is less developed, unions covering several provinces have been formed. For certain particular industries there are regional associations. Thus there are twelve regional groups of electrical undertakings, three regional *consortia* of mechanical and metallurgical industries, twenty-four federations of house owners. The confederations are the following:

Employers' Associations.

1. General Confederation of Industry.
2. General Confederation of Agriculture.
3. General Confederation of Commerce.
4. General Banking Confederation.
5. General Confederation of Land Transport and Inland Waterways.
6. General Confederation of Maritime and Air Transport.

Workers' Associations.

7. National Confederation of Industrial Syndicates.
8. National Confederation of Agricultural Syndicates.
9. National Confederation of Commercial Syndicates.
10. National Confederation of Banking Syndicates.
11. National Confederation of Land Transport and Inland Waterways Syndicates.
12. National Confederation of Seamen and Airmen.

Organization of Professional Men.

13. National Confederation of Professional Men and Artists.

Just as a firm may form part of several employers' unions, similarly, the same individual may belong to different syndicates. He may be the owner of a small piece of land and a tenant of another. Hence he joins both the association of landowners and that of tenants.

Certain classes of citizens are not entitled to constitute legally recognized syndicates. These are the employees of the state, the provinces, the communes, and other public bodies. Owing to the peculiar nature of their contracts with their employer (the state, the province, etc.), they cannot be on a footing of equality with the latter, as is the case of workers in private business. They may form associations with the object of studying and promoting their own professional collective interests, but the authorization of the state is required for the constitution of such associations.[10]

Other classes of public servants (officials of the Ministries of Foreign Affairs, the Colonies, the Interior, and the Corporations, and all members of the fighting service of whatever rank) are not entitled to form associations.

Associations constituted in Italy must not form part of international bodies and place themselves under their orders without the permission of the proper authorities, for it is considered that there should be only one foreign policy for Italy and that that is the foreign policy of the Government. Private associations, however important, cannot be allowed to conduct an independent foreign policy of

[10] In the case of other classes of citizens, any group is free to form an association, and the authority of the state is only required in order that such a body may secure legal recognition. Civil servants, on the other hand, must apply for permission of the state before they may even form their associations.

their own. But permission to join international bodies is not usually refused, and the representatives of the Italian employers and workers play an active part in the International Labor Organization.

Each confederation has the following organs:

1. The national congress, composed of delegates of the various provincial and interprovincial associations forming a part of it, selected for each congress in numbers proportionate to the number of members of each member-association and in accordance with its statutes. The president, the members of the governing body of the confederation, and the heads of the national unions and syndicates, are *de jure* members of the congress. The congress meets every three years, or oftener if necessary.

2. The governing body, composed of representatives of national category organizations and one representative of the National Association of War Disabled. The governing body carries out the decisions of the national congress and conducts business between the meetings of the latter.

3. The presidency, whose occupant is appointed by the congress and approved by the proper authorities.

The regulations of the Confederation of Professional Men and Artists are somewhat different from the others, as its associates are neither employers nor workers, and their economic relations are with the public.

II. COLLECTIVE LABOR CONTRACTS

Collective labor contracts are, of course, no novelty, even in Italy. But in the past they were not very numerous, and they were usually the outcome of long and bitter conflicts. Their clauses were often imposed by the arbitrary will of the stronger of the two parties in the dispute; it was consequently difficult to enforce respect for agreements stipulated under compulsion, and the party forced to accept the will of its stronger opponent inevitably did so with mental reservations. Nor were they applicable to any but the parties who stipulated them, so that there might be considerable numbers of workmen performing the same work as that done by the parties to the contract, but who, not being members of the same unions, did not benefit by that contract and were forced to work under less favorable conditions.

Today the organizations stipulating these contracts are legally recognized bodies, and the observance of the said agreements is compulsory. They are binding not only upon the members of the associations who have stipulated them, but on all who are represented by these associations, i.e., by all who within the territorial jurisdiction of the contracting syndicates are engaged in that particular trade or branch of trade; they are applicable to the whole of Italy, even to the most backward areas and the most primitive professions. Thus a national contract for shepherds has been recently concluded.

The earlier collective contracts were tariff and factory agreements of limited scope, whereas those of today cover relations between employers and workers in all aspects and constitute a regular law of labor conditions.

For a collective labor contract to be valid, it must fulfil certain conditions. The contract must have been stipulated by the properly qualified associations which must have given their consent in proper form. In some cases the consent of the corresponding associations of a higher grade is also required. The contract must not deal with labor relations already covered by enactments of the public administration (i.e., it must not concern the workers employed by the state or other public bodies), nor with personal or domestic service, and it must not contain clauses contrary to law.

The contract must cover such matters as its own duration, disciplinary regulations, the period of apprenticeship, hours of work, wages, weekly repose, annual holidays with pay, cases of dismissal without any fault of the worker, the transfer of a business from one employer to another, the treatment of the worker in case of sickness and of absence on account of military service.

A collective contract must conciliate the interests of employers and workers in such a manner as not to cause prejudice to production. To be fully valid it must be published, so that all concerned may know its provisions. It thus has the force of law and is applicable to all persons engaged in the particular occupation residing in the area within the jurisdiction of the syndicates concerned. But if a contract should press too heavily on a certain weaker business, exemptions and special conditions may in some cases be granted to these. On the other hand, a collective contract is not applicable to cases where an existing special contract previously concluded is more favorable to the workers.

Penalties for breaches of collective contracts are laid down by law, and the employer who violates his undertakings is liable to a fine of 100 to 5,000 lire and is legally responsible to the other party and to the syndicates which stipulated the contract, while the association to which he belongs may also be held responsible if it has failed to try to enforce the observance of the contract or has guaranteed such observance.

A large number of collective contracts have now been stipulated and their number increases day by day. Up to December 31, 1927, 2,821 contracts covering not more than one province have been stipulated; 1,744 in 1928; 1,156 in 1929; 1,535 in 1930; in all 7,256. Of these, 3,094 were general and covered all labor relations, while 4,162 covered wages alone; 2,674 had been published and had become law by December 31, 1930. By the same date 281 collective contracts applicable to the whole of Italy, or at least to several provinces, had also been stipulated and deposited at the Ministry of Corporations. There are still a few industries not covered by collective contracts, but their number is decreasing.

Breaches of contract between syndical associations are very rare, although they sometimes occur in individual cases.

III. THE LABOR COURTS

We have seen how from the beginnings of the Fascist labor organization the elimination of strikes and lockouts was attempted, and how even in the early days of the new *régime* such violent forms of action had rapidly diminished. It was, of course, realized that no system, however perfect, could do away with labor disputes altogether; but methods have been devised to prevent them from degenerating into suspensions of production which are injurious to the whole nation. Just as in all civilized societies private individuals have no right to take justice into their own hands, Fascist Italy considers that classes and categories of workers likewise have not that right, but must, like private individuals, appeal to the superior and impartial authority of the state as represented by the courts of law. Strikes and lockouts are regarded as luxuries which Italy cannot afford.

The corollary of this theory is the compulsory judicial solution of labor disputes, which constitutes one of the most radical innovations yet introduced into Italian legislation. Machinery has been provided whereby employers and workers may defend their own rights. Various forms of arbitration and conciliation had been devised before, in Italy and other countries, notably Germany, Australia, New Zealand, and some of the American states. But none of them have proved completely successful, or prevented occasional recourse to violence in the last resort, i.e., to strikes and lockouts.

In the Italian system there are two successive stages of procedure:

a. Conciliation by means of the syndical associations, the corporations or the Ministry of Corporations.

b. If conciliation fails, recourse to the Labor Court.

Conciliation is not strictly regulated by law, but is intrusted to the associations, which create the mixed committees *ad hoc* already alluded to, the corporations (when they exist), the Ministry of Corporations, and the other conciliatory organs, all of which enjoy considerable latitude in the methods for arriving at a settlement. If these attempts fail, the parties go before the Labor Court. Before such an appeal is allowed the conciliatory procedure must first have been tried and have failed. Even when the case comes before the Court, the President must make a final attempt to settle the dispute amicably before opening the legal proceedings, and during the course of these proceedings he must renew the attempt every time he sees a favorable opening.

The Labor Courts are not special tribunals, but sections of the existing Courts of Appeal. In each Court of Appeal, a Labor Court is formed to try labor cases as they arise, and is composed of three judges,[11] one a president of section, and two counselors of appeal, to whom two "assessors" are attached, one an expert on labor problems and one an expert on production problems. These assessors are selected from a panel existing in each district. Neither of them may have any personal interest in the case. They are not representatives of either side and must be neither employers nor workers, but are chosen as experts and form part of the court.

The Labor Court is competent to judge disputes between different categories of workers and employers concerning the observance and application of laws, the rules laid down in collective contracts, other provisions on labor conditions, and provisions arising out of a modification of the terms of the

---

[11] In Italy judges are public servants appointed by competitive examinations, who cannot be dismissed save for definite offenses of a grave nature, proved by a court of law or a disciplinary court, or even transferred from one court to another except for very serious reasons, although of course they may be transferred on promotion to higher rank in the service.

contract demanded by either side. Each Labor Court deals with disputes within its own district. The Rome Court is competent to try cases concerning several judicial districts.

The Court decides according to legislation, where it exists, and the Labor Charter, or, failing either, according to custom and equity. It is indeed, primarily an equity court. It can fix fair wages, and must in its decisions always bear in mind the necessity of a living wage for the worker, the economic possibilities of the employer, and the superior interests of production. Society's interest is that production should continue, and that its cost should not be so high as to prevent national industry from competing with that of other countries.

The Labor Court is not competent to try cases concerning private individuals; these are referred to the ordinary lower court to which two assessors are attached if the parties apply for them. Nor may it try cases involving non-recognized associations. It may try cases concerning a professional category for which no association exists or has been recognized, and in those circumstances the President of the Court appoints a guardian to represent the group concerned.

The public prosecutor himself may intervene directly, and may take the initiative in bringing a dispute before the Court if the parties concerned do not appeal and public interest requires that the case should be thrashed out in Court.

The awards delivered by the Labor Court have compulsory force. The employer or worker refusing to abide by them is liable to imprisonment from one month to one year and to a fine of from 100 to 5,000 lire. The punishment is more severe in the case of the executive of an association than in that of ordinary members.

As we have seen, strikes and lockouts have been declared illegal, because both are regarded as prejudicial to the whole community. A lockout is defined by law as the closing of a factory in order to force the workers to accept a modification of labor conditions, or for some other illicit purpose, while a strike is the suspension or the obstruction of work by at least three workers acting by previous agreement. The penalty for a lockout is a fine of 10,000 to 100,000 lire, for a strike of one hundred to one thousand. If the object for which the strike or lockout is proclaimed does not concern labor conditions, the fine is 500 lire for either employer or worker. If there is violence or physical constraint, the penalty is imprisonment and a fine of 100 to 3,000 lire. Organizers and promoters are more seriously punished than mere participants, and if the public authorities are prevented by the strikes and lockouts from carrying out their functions or public services are held up, severer penalties are likewise imposed.

The number of cases tried by the Labor Courts is small, whereas the number of labor contracts stipulated by the associations and that of the disputes settled by the organs of conciliation are very large. The provisions for punishing strikes and lockouts would not of themselves suffice, if public opinion were not now convinced that direct action must give way to a peaceful solution, and that the system evolved is on the whole the best for the country. The penalties have in fact hardly ever been applied, because the necessity for them has very seldom arisen.

An interesting case recently settled by the Labor Court is that arising out of a dispute between owners of rice fields in northern Italy and the women employed to weed the crop. Rice having been seriously affected by the fall in prices, the growers proposed a 45 per cent cut in the wages. The women, represented by their syndicate, admitted trade depression and were prepared to accept a reduction, but only one of not more than 20 per cent. After protracted discussion and many attempts at conciliation, the employers brought their claim down to a 30 per cent cut, which the syndicates would not accept. Finally the case was referred to the Labor Court, which, after a full public inquiry into the conditions of the market and the necessities of the workers, issued an award reducing wages by 24 per cent, but also reducing the sums retained by the growers for the meals supplied to the workers, so that the actual reduction of the wages was 22 per cent. The dispute was thus settled without friction and without the loss of a single day's work.

The system is gradually coming to be taken for granted, and although breaches of these provisions may no doubt occur in the future, they will end by being regarded in the same light as breaches of the law.

IV. THE CORPORATIONS

The existence of separate associations for the various categories of producers required the creation of liaison organs linking them up. These were to have been the corporations, state institutions grouping all associations interested in a particular branch of economic activity and fulfilling the functions of organs of conciliation for the settlement of labor disputes. The corporations were only sketched out in the law of April 3, 1926, but by the law of March 20, 1930, the National Council of Corporations was created, a composite body on which many institutions, departments, and interests are represented; it is divided into sections, which operate at present as corporations, taking the place of the mixed committees previously mentioned.

The National Council was created to coördinate all the productive forces of the nation in conformity with the Sixth Declaration of the Labor Charter. The mixed committees first gave practical expression to the idea of class collaboration, but the corporations are to encourage and direct it, and the National Council coördinates the corporations. The chairman of the Council is the Prime Minister, who may, and usually does, delegate his authority to the Minister of Corporations. The members comprise certain members of the Cabinet, high officials, delegates of the various recognized syndical organizations in numbers proportionate to their importance, the representatives of the employers and of the workers being in equal numbers, and ten experts.

While the various confederations represent the joint interests of a whole class of either employers or workers, the corporations are to group both employers and workers in a particular branch of industry or commerce; it is their function to study conflicts of interest, the possibilities of expansion, development, costs of production, etc. The Council is further intrusted with the duty of coördinating the interests of the various branches of trade; this is a particularly important provision, and implies the settling of such conflicts as may arise, as for instance between agriculture and industry, or between two or more rival industries.

The corporations also deal with employment and may provide employment bureaus of their own, composed of employees' and workers' delegates in equal numbers. Where such public bureaus exist, private employment agencies, in conformity with the resolutions of the Washington Labor Conference, are suppressed, and employers must select their own workers from its lists.

The National Council has its provincial organs in the Provincial Councils of Economy, which have been transformed into provincial corporations covering all branches of industry in each province.

Up to the present the corporations have not been created, except the National Corporation of the Theater. Others will be created in due course, but in the meanwhile their duties are being carried out by the sections of the National Council, each section of which is composed of delegates of the various confederations and associations concerned.

As Signor Bottai said in his speech in the Chamber of Deputies (December 21, 1929) in the debate on the constitution of the Council, this body is not a parliament, nor is it merely a department of the Ministry of Corporations. It is a national organ of the state designed to hold the balance between the syndicates and private enterprise.

It has been often asserted that the Italian system is but a form of state Socialism, and that it tends to hinder and finally to absorb all forms of private enterprise. But this idea is erroneous; the Labor Charter, which inspires the whole body of legislation and practice in Italian labor and production, is based on four main motives; private enterprise, syndical activity, corporative activity, and state intervention. Signor Bottai pointed out in the same speech that if you suppress private enterprise you have syndical tyranny, which will undermine the moral and social structure of the state; if you suppress syndical action, you destroy those intermediate organizations conceived by Fascism in contrast to traditional Liberal economy; if you suppress corporative action, you isolate the syndicates in the arid wastes of mere labor disputes; if you do away with state intervention altogether, you have once more the struggle between individual anarchy and syndicalism which characterized Italian economic life in the past.

V. THE MINISTRY OF CORPORATIONS

This Ministry, whose officials were mostly selected from other Ministries and departments, is a kind of super-liaison organ designed to coördinate various activities converging on the corporations. Originally it dealt only with matters directly concerning the corporative system and its organization, but it has now taken over many of the duties of the suppressed Ministry of National Economy (except those concerning agriculture, for which a special Ministry exists).

Political Representation.

The corporative system plays an important rôle in the reformed political constitution of Italy. The commission of eighteen had prepared a scheme for a partial corporative Parliament—one of the two Chambers was to remain purely political and the other to embody the syndical organizations. But actually effect was given to this proposal only in a modified form. The composition of the Senate remains unchanged. The Chamber of Deputies is elected in a manner in which the syndicates have a share instead of by geographical constituencies. Each of the general confederations and certain other legally recognized organizations propose the names of a number of candidates, one thousand in all. The Fascist Grand Council selects four hundred names out of the thousand, or it may choose a slightly smaller number, bringing the total up to four hundred with the addition of a few names of men of high standing and merit not connected with any existing organization, but whose collaboration is deemed useful. The four hundred names are submitted to the electorate which votes for or against the whole list. If the list secures a majority of the votes, it is elected *en bloc;* if it is in a minority, new elections are held on the system of proportional representation, any organization of five thousand voters being authorized to present a list of its own.

At the first election held under the new system, the list prepared by the Grand Council was voted by an overwhelming majority, and the Chamber contains representatives of the various confederations and other organizations in different proportions according to their relative importance. The thirteen confederations are represented by two hundred members; each confederation of employers having the same number of representatives as the corresponding confederation of workers. Thus the Con-

federation of Agriculture is represented by twenty-
four members, and the Confederation of Agricultural Workers by a similar number; the Employers'
Confederation of Industry by twenty members, and
the Workers' Confederation of Industry also by
twenty members, and the same proportions are
maintained in the others. The Confederation of Professional Men and Artists returns forty members, a
provision which stresses the importance attached to
intellectual activity in the new system. Another aspect of Fascism is stressed by the presence of forty-
five members selected out of a list presented by the
ex-service men's association, and thirty out of that
of the disabled war veterans.

The dominant idea is that the citizen has the right
to take part in the selection of candidates not because he is a citizen of twenty-one years of age, but
because he is a producer and belongs to some recognized association; at the actual election, on the
other hand, the citizens vote as individuals. The election itself is more in the nature of a plebiscite than
an election in the ordinary meaning of the term. The
voter is called upon to express his approval or dis-
approval of the whole policy carried out by the Government during its five years' tenure of office. Even
if the Government were to secure a majority of the
votes, but were to find a strong minority against it,
this result would be tantamount to a partial criticism of its action, and would presumably lead to a
partial change in the trend of its policy.

The electoral system, like the corporative system
with which it is associated, is not regarded as final,
but as an experiment. A permanent commission has
been appointed to study its workings and to report

from time to time on the manner in which it operates, and if necessary suggest improvements. Revision is therefore possible and even probable. What hardly anyone wants is a reversion to the unsatisfactory methods of the past. The old Liberal Constitution and the party system, which have had their uses and rendered good service to the country in former years, are now regarded as obsolete, and a return to them is highly improbable. Above all, the old attitude of the state which ignored labor and labor conflicts and allowed class to wage war against class is, all Italians believe and hope, a thing of the past.

I need not dwell on the political aspects of the system, which are outside the scope of my lecture, beyond stating that it is essentially the outcome of Italian conditions. Some of its aspects may, no doubt, be imitated elsewhere, but Italy does not require foreign imitations. This indeed is one of the cardinal differences between Fascism and Bolshevism. If Bolshevism is not adopted by other countries besides Russia, it appears improbable that it can survive even there, unless it is greatly modified. Hence the vast effort at propaganda to convert other countries to the Bolshevik idea. Fascism may think that other countries will end by adopting certain Fascist principles and institutions, but whether this occurs or not, it will not affect the Italian experiment in itself, and is not in any way necessary for its success in Italy.

I may be asked how the new reforms have worked out in practice. The corporative system is only in its beginnings, and not yet, by any means, fully evolved. As I said before, most of the corporations have still to be created; the syndicates and associations have not yet gathered in the whole producing population, and while they are highly developed and functioning satisfactorily in some areas of the country, in certain trades and in certain classes of workers, they have still to be perfected in others.

Given the short time in which the system has been in existence, a definite verdict on it cannot yet be pronounced, especially as its beginnings have coincided with the world economic crisis. I may say, however, that the following results have been obtained.

1. All strikes and lockouts have been eliminated and innumerable labor disputes settled peaceably without leaving a trail of bitterness behind them.

2. The conditions of labor in the more backward and poorer parts of Italy are tending to attain the standards of the more advanced parts. Collective contracts for agricultural labor in Sicily and other areas of the south, which even the Socialists had failed to secure, are now realized.

3. In the first years of the Fascist *régime* production continued to increase in quantity and to improve in quality both as compared with 1913 and with the years immediately following the war before the development of the new system, until the effects of the world crisis reached Italy, namely, in the course of 1930. Today the depression is felt in the general fall of prices, which have been particularly serious in certain forms of agriculture; there has been a reduction of output in domestic trade and foreign trade, and an increase of unemployment. Unemployment, however, is in smaller proportions than in most of the other leading countries. Out of a

total population of 42,000,000 inhabitants, the maximum unemployment in the winter months of 1931 was somewhat under 800,000; on July 1 of this year it had fallen to 575,000.[12] In Italy the partially seasonal character of unemployment is particularly marked. These figures are in themselves not excessive and it should be borne in mind that in the years preceding the crisis unemployment fell as low as 78,000. Moreover, there has been in the last eight or nine years a very considerable reduction in emigration as compared with the years preceding the war and those immediately following it. While in 1919–22 unemployment had averaged between 500,000 and 600,000, emigration was at about the same figure. Today, with unemployment between 500,000 and 800,000, emigration is only between 180,000 and 300,000. Nor should we forget that the endemic strikes of 1919–22 may be regarded as an additional form of unemployment, and these have now been definitely eliminated. Thus a larger number of persons are employed in Italy than was the case ten or twelve years ago.

Finally, owing to the world economic depression Italy now finds herself burdened with a part of the unemployed of some other lands, as represented by those of her own citizens who habitually emigrate or reside abroad, but have repatriated on account of the depression in other countries. Many of the persons who would otherwise be registered as unemployed in the United States and France are today to be found in Italy, while others are in Poland, Czechoslovakia, Hungary, etc.

4. Italy's unemployment policy is based on a

[12] By the end of 1931 the figure was approaching one million.

measure of unemployment insurance combined with works of public utility calculated to increase the national income. Both the Government and other public bodies make every effort to employ as large a number of persons as possible on land reclamation, road-building, hydro-electric development, etc., in order to avoid creating a class of persons permanently unemployed. While economies are being effected in every branch of the public service, exceptions are made even now for land reclamation and road-building. Land reclamation is of peculiar importance for Italy's existence, as the country has a comparatively small area of fertile land, and a part of that land cannot be fully exploited on account of drought, floods, and malaria. The land reclamation policy of the present Government is on a more systematic and coördinated scale than that of its predecessor. A good deal of reclamation work had indeed been carried out in the past, but in an incomplete form and in a piecemeal fashion, because the Government was unable to resist the pressure of innumerable demands from all parts of the country where reclamation works were, or were supposed to be, desirable. The present administration is strong enough to concentrate its activities on those areas where reclamation is really essential and to carry out its schemes in a complete manner. The Government does not defray the whole cost of these schemes. It carries out at its own expense only works of general public utility, such as drainage and irrigation canals, roads, etc., and advances loans on easy terms to the landowners for those works which are of some special interest to their own properties.

This may be regarded as a form of state intervention or national planning. It is, however, no novelty in Italy. Legislation has existed for many decades, imposing on landowners, in one form or another, the obligation to cultivate their land adequately. Where compulsory reclamation laws exist, as in the case of the Roman Campagna, the owners are called upon to carry out the schemes laid down by the agricultural authorities for drainage, irrigation, the building of houses, silos, barns, and stables, the construction of roads, etc. Landowners failing to carry out their obligations under these laws are liable to penalties extending from fines to expropriation in the public interest. Under the present *régime* such provisions have been strengthened and their execution has been enforced with greater rigor.

It should be remembered that, as Senator Conti pointed out in his report to the Senate on May 9, 1931, "Italian economy has borne itself and continues to bear itself in a wholly satisfactory manner in view of the difficult situation created by the world crisis." Italy has undoubtedly felt the effects of the depression, but in a degree of intensity less acute than in some other countries, and it is being supported with a spirit of national collaboration which would not have been possible under any other system. Senator Conti adds that

to this have contributed the spirit of enterprise and discipline and national solidarity which Fascism promotes and diffuses throughout all the strata of all classes of Italian people, and the vigorous, careful, and efficient action which the Government carries out either directly or by means of the corporative organizations to sustain, stimulate and promote national economic activity, encourage enterprise, and prevent all relaxation of that tenacious will to victory which is the first condition of resistance in the present adversities and of happily overcoming them.

Without the corporative system and the spirit which it has engendered, it would have been impossible to enact the measures necessary to meet the crisis without provoking serious labor conflicts and strikes and a recrudescence of class war.

In the years 1922–27, when business was doing well after the stagnation and disastrous anarchy of the previous years, the *régime* promoted an increase of wages. With the advent of the world depression it has been necessary to curtail public expenditures. The Government began by cutting down the salaries of its own employees by 12½ per cent, and the other public bodies followed suit. Business undertakings whose earnings had been curtailed also cut down wages; this went into effect as a result of negotiations with the workers. At the same time the Government and the other public bodies both by direct action and through the syndical organizations developed an active policy of price reduction. Rents have been reduced by 10 per cent in practically every city of Italy. The general reduction of retail prices has not quite corresponded to the reduction of wages, but is approaching it. The reductions have more particularly benefited the poorer classes, while the wealthier ones are expected to make more sacrifices, as they are better able to bear them.

By the economies thus effected the Government has been able to reduce the budget deficit, which at the end of the fiscal year amounted to about $45,-000,000.

5. While reducing expenses, the Government has

continued its policy of restricting borrowing abroad.
Only two municipalities have been allowed to contract loans with foreign governments—Rome and
Milan. The foreign borrowings of private undertakings have also been restricted. As the short-term
Treasury bonds fall due in November, 1931, many
rumors had been circulated abroad concerning the
issue of a new foreign loan for that purpose. But in
actual fact the Government not only did not apply
for such a loan, but refused various offers of loans
which were made to it by different foreign financial
groups. An internal loan was floated instead last
spring to cover the coming payments. The sum applied for was 4,000,000 lire; actually 7,000,000 were
subscribed, and the Government refused to accept
more than 5,000,000. The small amount of Italy's
foreign indebtedness is indeed of great value in
helping the country through the depression.

The system has encountered many obstacles. Not
all individuals or groups accept it unquestioningly.
A few attempts at evasion of the labor contracts
have been made by employers, but they are not numerous. As I have said before, the masses have not
everywhere joined the syndicates in the same proportions. Adhesion has been less marked in some
cases than in others. In industry the membership of
the associations, both of employers and workers,
has been larger than in other branches of economic
activity. In the north where trade-unionism had
been developed for decades, the new system was better understood than in the south.

In agriculture and commerce applications for

membership have been less numerous, particularly in the case of the small holders and small shopkeepers. Italy is becoming more and more a land of small holders and is still a land of small shopkeepers.[13] In some cases workers have failed to join the syndicates because, although they enjoy the protection of the syndicates and must pay their contributions even if not members, those who become members are called upon, as said before, to pay additional fees for membership cards, etc. While admission to the Fascist party is closed save to those who have passed through the youth organizations, adherence to the syndicates is encouraged.

Another difficulty is that certain undesirable elements have penetrated into the syndicates, and some converted Socialists and even Communists have joined, with their complete baggage of demagogic spirit. But these are defects which time will correct. Nor is it always easy to find suitable men to act as presidents and secretaries of the syndicates; a remedy is being sought by the institution of courses for "syndical leaders," where young men are trained to the duties for the carrying out and development of the system as secretaries of syndicates.

The question which is often asked is whether Fascist economy is a challenge to other systems, notably to Communism and Capitalism. The Fascist system undoubtedly offers a sharp contrast to Communism, and may be regarded as its direct opposite. Communism is based on the predominance, both in politics and in economics, of one class—the proletariat—and, indeed, of a minority of that class.

[13] Large department stores and chain stores are not popular.

Fascism, as I have shown, is definitely a system of class collaboration. It rejects the idea of class and of contrast between classes, and aims at conciliating the aspirations of all the categories of the population in the interests of the nation as a whole.

Does it challenge capitalism? If by capitalism we mean simply the classical liberal economic theory of *laissez faire*,[14] Fascism does represent a new spirit, inasmuch as it provides for a form of economic planning which in some quarters is regarded as tantamount to a kind of state Socialism. But if by capitalism we mean individual enterprise and the possession of the means of production by private individuals and undertakings, Fascism by no means rejects it. In Fascist economics the state steps in only to correct the defects and deficiencies of private enterprise and intervenes where private enterprise has failed. But the capitalist principle is accepted. Mussolini in fact stated that an extension of capitalist organization to Africa and Asia was desirable, in the interest of world economic development.

In a country as poor in natural resources as Italy, a form of national economic discipline such as that laid down by Fascism is indispensable, for without it the resources she possesses cannot be exploited to the full.

As Professor Bodrero stated in a recent speech to the General Confederation of Professional Men, of which he is President: "By means of our new conception of the corporative state, it is inconceivable that anyone should be in the future an ab-

[14] There is a certain looseness of thought which confuses the two ideas.

solutely free owner, in the old sense of the word, but everyone may and shall be an owner inasmuch as the exercise of his rights serves the nation.''

Then what of the future? The economic system of Fascism is closely bound up with the political aspects of the movement. According to some authorities, the economic aspect is destined to absorb the political one, and the Fascist state is likely to become more and more exclusively a corporative state. Be that as it may, both are undergoing a process of evolution and settlement, and neither has yet reached the goal. Both are inspired by the same principle of national collaboration, and on this point there can, I think, be no going back. Just as in international politics we must strive to secure a better understanding of the different national points of view and a closer collaboration between nations— and we are indeed progressing toward this aspiration—so in social economics, we should aim at a similar collaboration between all sections of the people. Interclass peace is just as important for the welfare of the community as international peace, and the one is a help toward the other.

In Italy class peace has been achieved. It is our aim and hope to contribute as much as lies within our power also toward peace among nations.

THE ECONOMICS OF CAPITALISM

BY MALCOLM C. RORTY

THE ECONOMICS OF CAPITALISM

I. POLITICAL AND ECONOMIC EVOLUTION

I AM to set forth here the standpoint of individualistic capitalism, to supplement the descriptions of the Soviet and Fascist systems previously presented by Dr. Counts and Professor Villari.

These discussions might readily have taken the form of a partisan debate between proponents of these several systems. Such a debate would, however, be very inopportune in these days when the world is so chastened by adversity and is so anxiously seeking the solution of its many difficulties.

In view of these conditions, I shall not, for my own part, attempt either to defend individualistic capitalism or to attack the state capitalism of the Russian Government or that special system of political and economic discipline represented by Fascism. Rather, I shall attempt to establish the general principles of political and economic organization, and to indicate, so far as possible, the natural and necessary lines along which such organization may evolve.

In considering the facts which underlie and govern the whole of social organization, our first problem is to determine, so far as we may, its real ends and purposes. The prime question is what we as human beings may reasonably ask and expect of society, not only for ourselves, but even more particularly for our children and our grandchildren.

In this respect I am reminded of the story told at

the expense of a very genial and human old lawyer of my acquaintance. This lawyer, at the solicitation of an old associate, engaged the services of his friend's son, Tommy, who turned out in due course to be perhaps the world's worst office boy. The situation soon passed endurance, and my friend was torn between an accumulating distaste for Tommy and a great hesitation to hurt the feelings of Tommy's father. At this juncture, he discovered that Tommy had realized the growing tension of the situation and had made application for a position with another lawyer, who wrote asking for information as to Tommy's qualifications.

Here was a problem that called for all the subtleties of the legal profession. My lawyer friend was by nature a very upright person, but he could not bring himself to forego this heaven-sent opportunity to rid himself of Tommy. So he struggled manfully with his conscience, and finally wrote, "My dear Mr. Jones: With reference to your letter just received, I would say that, if you are looking for an office boy like Tommy, then Tommy is exactly the office boy you want."

Now, the application of this tale to the present occasion lies in the fact that if we desire for ourselves, and for our children and our grandchildren, a system of state capitalism, or Fascism, or of individualistic capitalism, then, according to our desires, each particular system may be exactly what we want.

However, so nimble a solution is no permanent answer to our present difficulties. We cannot thus easily avoid the real problems of searching for some common measures of human values and of determining how far the existing political and economic systems may be capable of realizing such values, and what the trend of social evolution will probably be in the direction of their further realization.

In attempting to determine these fundamental values, our initial consideration is of method of approach.

We may, I believe, agree that whatever values we establish must be those that relate to a vigorous, growing, and self-perpetuating society, rather than to individual desires. It is undoubtedly the privilege of the individual to detach himself from the main stream of social evolution and to establish, so far as he may, his own particular scale of values and his own particular plan of life. But, if he so detaches himself, he should, in all due sanity and modesty, not attempt to speak for society as a whole in terms of his special scheme of things. Whatever social values we establish must at least be concordant with the perpetuation of the society and with its vigorous and unhampered evolution.

We may, however, go a step further, in establishing the background for our determination of social values, by recognizing frankly that we are dealing with an evolutionary process, as applied to which the best of our individual wisdom is futile and untrustworthy, when compared with the accumulated and instinctive biological wisdom of hundreds of thousands of years. Our search for social values must not, therefore, bring us the product of our own individual desires and imaginations, but must lead us rather to determine as accurately as we can, from the past history and present trends of mankind, those objectives which are inherent in the nature of human evolution. The less we impose of our own desires and our own theories, and the more accurately we observe the facts as they have been, and are, and tend to be, the nearer we shall come to the truth.

Let me emphasize this point. The most precious possession of a nation is the idealism of its people— and the greatest loss a nation can suffer is the waste of this idealism in vain plans and vain efforts based on false and erroneous premises. Our problem is not to plan the social millennium, but, with Emerson, to "accept the universe," and to do, from time to time, the reasonably good thing that can be done, rather than to struggle vainly for an impossible perfection.

If, then, we approach our search for fundamental human values from a strictly evolutionary and historical point of view, our first clear concept is that nature is quite as willing to people the earth with Hottentots as with Caucasians. She recognizes no racial values except the value of racial survival. Her only test of fitness to survive is ability to do so.

In the processes of organic development, nature reveals a series of transitions from the lowest organisms that have no family life, through forms of a somewhat higher type that have a family life but no social life, to the highest organisms, including man, that have both family and social lives.

In this long scale of evolution, it is apparent that each step in social development, through the animal family to the fully organized human tribe or nation, has served its purpose in facilitating survival. Family life gives protection to the growing generation; social life gives further support to the individual and, in addition, organizes the tribe as a whole for defense against inroads from without, or for forays into neighboring territory.

In the soundly evolved society, there is an instinctive compromise between the individual and the community. The individual sacrifices the unessentials of individual liberty for the essentials of community benefits; and, in the reverse direction, the society yields the unessentials of social unity to the preservation of the essential values of individual freedom.

This compromise is based upon no theories as to the relative values of social powers and individual liberties. The only test is racial survival. The race that too far subordinates the individual to society may gain temporarily in strength of common purpose, but loses, ultimately, through the stifling of individual powers of growth and development. There are no bee or antlike animals in the family tree of mankind—although, in the reverse direction, the race that is too individualistic for social coöperation tends always to give way in direct competition with more highly organized groups.

The special characteristics of evolutionary progress are, as might be expected, exemplified to their highest degree in the records of mankind. Both history and prehistoric evidence indicate a succession of racial movements, usually under pressure of overpopulation and food shortage, whereby the more vigorous races, that were better organized and more powerful in war, overran and dispossessed their neighbors. Regardless of sentimental objections, the glorification of the military virtues in history has its absolute evolutionary justification.

It would, however, be a perversion of the facts to end here with a statement that human values and the value of social system must be measured today primarily and directly in terms of their contributions to racial or national power in war. Evolution is still in progress, and the greatest single step in human evolution has come, perhaps, in very recent years, with the attainment, or approaching attainment, of a stabilization in size of the populations of the leading civilized countries. With this great change has come a further equally important change in the growing and conscious recognition of the fact (which instinctively we have always known) that unity and homogeneity of population are essential features of racial and national strength.

If I may digress for a moment, there has been much confusion and half-thinking in this latter respect. Our hopes and our plans can rarely run beyond a century. We are fortunate if we can think constructively even ten years ahead. It may be true that racial differences are insignificant when measured in the scale of geologic time, and that ten thousand years ago our ancestors were inferior to any of the races we should now rate low in the human scale, or that ten thousand years hence the blacks or the Red Indians may be the leaders of civilization. Such periods are, however, too long for our consciousness or our instincts to recognize. What we know instinctively today, and what only a perverted sentimentalism prevents us from recognizing consciously and universally, is that there are racial differences which, for all practical purposes and for all practical time, are permanent and unchangeable.

No capable farmer fails to plant purely bred seed,

THE ECONOMICS OF CAPITALISM 121

or to fertilize and cultivate his crops. He has no il-
lusions as to the relative importance of heredity and
environment in the outcome of his efforts, nor does
he expect good cultivation to take the place of good
seed, or good seed the place of cultivation.

So, in the cultivation of our human crops, we
know instinctively that there are fundamental differences in racial quality. We know, also, that regardless of the absolute level of quality of any
population, the soundness of its society depends in
great part upon its degree of unity in race and traditions and ideals, and upon the absence of those
fixed class barriers that tend to grow up when unity
is lacking. Our accumulated biological wisdom tells
us, furthermore, that a certain element of racial
pride and of intolerance toward racial or social admixtures is one true measure of racial and social
vigor. We do not need an elaboration of scientific
reasons against racial admixtures—the instinctive
reason is, in itself, the soundest and most scientific.
We obtain the complete and absolute answer when
we ask ourselves with what races, or into what
groups, we should be willing or unwilling for our
sons and our daughters to marry.

With this accentuation of race consciousness, to
which I have just referred, and with the trend
toward stabilization of numbers, we are apparently
approaching a new stage in the development of the
world's populations. The old era of mass movements
of peoples is ending. A new era of stabilized and increasingly homogeneous populations in the great
civilized countries is beginning.

When the history of these times is finally written,
we may find that the Great War will be noted only

as a contributing incident to this greater event. For our present purposes, however, the important point is that this change carries with it certain radical changes in those factors which determine human and social evolution.

The theory of armed aggression as an instrument of civilized state policy is coming, by evolutionary processes, to its natural end. The Kellogg Treaty does not create a fact—it simply recognizes one that is in the making.

As a substitute for armed aggression we have now the theory of mandates for uncivilized and disorganized territories—although the semicivilized countries (define them as you will) constitute, in the society of nations, a problem quite similar to that of the semi-inferior elements of population in a single country. Obviously inferior racial elements can be socially segregated to do no great harm, just as the wholly uncivilized countries can be controlled by mandate. But the semi-inferior racial strain permeates the blood stream and the social life of a people like a virulent disease.

It would be idle, of course, to say that we have seen the last of wars. Minor foreign wars we shall certainly have. Major foreign wars are still not impossible. And civil wars and violent internal political struggles may continue for all time that we can measure. But the world-wide tendency toward a stabilization of human numbers indicates a definite change in evolutionary trend upon which we may base new measures of human values. The frontier days of civilization are ending. The power of the international bad man is passing. The vigilance committee of nations that fought the Great War cannot

shirk, in the end, its further responsibility for the
establishment of a new *régime* of international law
and order.

What will be the processes of human evolution
under these new conditions? The picture cannot be
wholly definite, but it may be possible to trace at
least its broader outlines.

First of all, that part of the evolutionary process
which has depended in the past upon the overrun-
ning, or dispossession, or partial or complete ex-
termination of one people by another, will sink into
unimportance.

In the second place, the conflicts of dynasties and
their related social system for possession of the
waste spaces of the earth are vanishing with the
simultaneous vanishing of the dynasties and the
waste spaces. It is true that the passing of kingly
power has raised up a new crop of dictators in those
countries that were not yet ripe for popular government. But these dictators have, on the whole, been
of a singularly benevolent type (as witness the late
Primo de Rivera), and the new world circumstances
have given them little temptation to resort to the old
expedient of foreign wars to draw as a red herring
across the trail of domestic difficulties. Even the
present Russian government seems to be in process
of recognizing that the world is well satisfied to let
it work out its own problems in its own way, and
asks only an equal tolerance and noninterference in
return. Only in Italy, among the great nations, has
Mussolini continued to talk of an ever expanding
population and of national rights to foreign territory for the needs of its overflow of numbers.

Sanity is but the infinitesimal point of balance

between an infinite range of insanities—and it would
be vain optimism to hope for a saner and more
peaceful world, if it did not seem that the roads of
international peace were now the natural roads of
evolution. A true League of Nations cannot be created, but the vitality of the idea, in spite of all obstacles, is the best indication that a natural League
of Nations will continue to evolve.

Whatever may be the nominal conditions of membership in such a league, a full and genuine standing for any country will involve a present or
ultimate stabilization in size of population; a recognition of reciprocal national rights to regulate immi-
gration; an equal recognition of reciprocal rights
to regulate commerce by tariffs or otherwise, subject to the limitation that no action shall be taken
to cause violent or sudden changes in established
trade currents; and, finally, a complete and sincere
abandonment of armed aggression and political
propaganda abroad as basic elements of state
policy.

This completes our rough picture of the fundamental and very recent changes that are in process
in political and social evolution. The major human
races and the major national strains of today may
be counted upon to survive and to evolve as individuals, but the human evolution of the future
should, nevertheless, be very largely the evolution
of social systems. The systems that meet the requirements of the new international obligations that have
been indicated, and that develop and maintain their
internal unities, will survive. Those that fail to do
so will pass away. Here, once again, the test of value
is purely that of ability to endure—and we may,

perhaps, sum up our analysis to this point by concluding that the fundamental and enduring values in any future social system will be those that contribute to national unity, to strength in defense against outside aggression, and to a sane, patient, tolerant, and non-aggressive foreign policy.

In the present world we still have remnants of the traditional governments—the old kingdoms and empires. We have a crop of dictators to replace traditional governments that have fallen, or popular governments that have failed. And we have even a surviving remnant of the old theological empires. But, for the immediate future, our interest very properly centers in the contest of ideas between three great systems—popular governments with their individualistic capitalism; the politico-economic dictatorship of Mussolini and the Fascist party in Italy; and the system of state capitalism represented by the present dictatorial Russian government.

If our previous analysis is sound, the ultimate survival of these three systems will be determined, first, by their ability to live in peace with their neighbors, and secondly, by their ability to satisfy natural human instincts to the degree necessary to develop and maintain internal unity, either in their present forms, or in the forms which they may evolve.

For our present purposes we may, perhaps, disregard the problem of foreign relations. The Russian Government has recently announced its belief that it can develop its own system effectively without the concurrence of a world revolution against capitalism—and even Mussolini, according to the latest rumors, may in time accept the principle of birth control.

Dictatorships of whatever kind—whether of individuals, or of organized parties, or of fanatically held ideas and ideals—have their serious weaknesses and their serious possibilities of creating foreign complications, which tend to be avoided by popular governments by reason of their many checks and balances. We may assume, however, that, if the existing Russian and Italian governments succeed in establishing true internal unity, those present elements of dictatorship which might contribute to foreign complications will become subordinated in due time to the need for a more thoroughgoing popular control of internal affairs.

On the preceding assumption we may properly confine ourselves to considering, for each of the three systems, those elements that relate to internal development and to the satisfaction of natural and instinctive human desires. The measure of evolutionary value with which we are concerned is that of national unity, but national unity can exist only when a people as a whole have an abiding conviction of the usefulness and worthiness of their social order. Furthermore, the nation that establishes a true internal unity will, almost of necessity, combine with that unity an adequate strength for the purposes of defense against outside aggression.

From this point we may proceed at once to a very simple and crucial further consideration. The primary desires of man are economic, and to obtain an irreducible minimum of economic satisfactions he will accept almost any form of social organization. The necessities of life are the first demand—but let these necessities once be satisfied, and the next demand is not for absolute liberty, but for specific liberties—for the right of each man to pursue happiness in his own way so long as he does not infringe upon the equal rights of his neighbors.

This is the simple, complete, and ultimate answer to the problem of governmental and economic systems that now confronts us. If, as seems quite possible, each of the three systems—the system of individualistic capitalism, the Russian system of state capitalism, and the politico-economic dictatorship of Fascism—can in due time supply an adequate and continuously assured minimum of economic needs to populations stabilized within the supporting limits of natural resources, each in turn will find the dominating demands of its people thereafter to be not so much for further economic satisfactions as for further liberties. Any system may permanently survive, or all three systems may survive, if, once having satisfied primary economic needs, it can equally satisfy the demand for human liberties.

In considering the natural demand for human liberties, it will simplify our discussion to make an initial distinction between liberties that are primarily economic and those that are more purely political.

Primitive political freedom can exist only in the case of nomadic populations. The beginnings of agricultural civilizations, which tied man to their crops and the soil, brought, also, the beginnings of organized, and almost invariably despotic, government.

Political liberties, as we know them, have been matters of slow evolution; and it is possible to trace back the forms of representative popular govern-

ment that are best exemplified, perhaps, in the
United States and the British Empire, in an un-
broken course for a thousand years or more, to their
beginnings in that feudal system with which organized government began to rebuild itself after the
downfall of the Roman Empire. From these beginnings, the sequence was an orderly and logical one—
robber barons, absolute monarchies, constitutional
monarchies, and finally the gradual development of
parliamentary forms and of representative popular
government as we know them today.

In this whole course of political evolution, the outstanding lesson has been that any form of election
or succession of the rulers or ruling group has been
good that has made the rulers truly representative
of the balance of power in the community. The first
essential in government was stability, and this could
result only from responsiveness to the true power of
the people.

Representative popular government can exist
soundly only when in logical fulfilment of this basic
requirement. It had its origins, as we know, in the
gradually declining disparity between the military
power of the commoner and that of the knight in
armor. The theory of popular government and of
universal suffrage has, however, its fundamental
defect in that it assumes that a count of noses is a
count of power. There is and can be no such thing
as the right to vote—there can only be the power to
vote—and, if we should carry our political theories
to their ultimate conclusion, we should have plural
or fractional voting according to the power, or, if
you please, the worthiness, of each individual citizen.

The trend of popular government is, nevertheless, everywhere and apparently of necessity, toward universal suffrage on the basis of a single vote for each adult citizen. In countries with universal education, with homogeneous populations, and without serious class, religious, economic, or racial barriers, the system of popular government works out surprisingly well, in spite of its theoretical defects. In such countries there appears to be a natural tendency toward a two-party organization, which has the peculiar, and I think generally unrecognized, advantage that it tends to divide the ignorant vote into approximately equal portions between the two parties, thus politically sterilizing such vote and leaving actual political control to the more intelligent voters who from time to time will shift their political allegiance.

On the other hand, the democratic theory, if we please to call it that, breaks down more or less completely in countries that are divided into discordant racial, social, religious, or economic groups, or are lacking in universality of education or in natural capacity for organized effort. In such countries the practice of democracy is too far removed from the fundamental requirement that the control of government shall lie in the hands of the balance of worthiness and capacity of the community. Each individual group tends to organize its separate political party, the suffrage of the ignorant becomes effective, and the interests of the people as a whole are lost in a tangle of temporary and shifting compromise between these special groups.

These peculiarities of popular government have been brought into strong relief by the events following the Great War. The orderly evolution of many governments, through the stage of hereditary rule to more democratic forms, has been interrupted by the discrediting of kingly power. The responsibilities of popular government have been thrown upon peoples not yet ripe or trained for such responsibilities. A reversion to hereditary rule was not in the order of events. The necessary result has been the raising up of a new crop of dictators—some openly avowing themselves as such, others professing allegiance to a selected electorate organized as a close-knit political party, and still others holding power under the outward forms of popular elections.

With the discrediting of kingly power, the world of today has, in fact, a choice only between popular governments for capable and united peoples and dictatorships for those that are incapable or disunited.

The majority of these dictators, including, I believe, Stalin and Mussolini, are conscientious men seeking to do the best that they can for the ultimate good of the peoples they rule. In most cases, they are dictators not so much from their own choice as from the necessities of circumstances that have made dictatorships inevitable as the only alternative to governmental chaos.

The theory of absolute dictatorship is not complicated. It is to subsidize adequately the army and the secret police; to win over those pretenders to power who can be conciliated; and to kill, banish, or imprison at the right time those pretenders who are unduly obstinate or grasping. With this primary procedure must also be combined, in these days, an organized control of the public press and of education, and an organized propaganda in glorification of the dictatorship. And, finally, of course, the dictatorship must be reasonably effective in furthering the economic needs of the country and in avoiding those spontaneous popular revolts that spring from absolute privation or from the laying of too obvious and heavy a hand upon the ordinary lives of the people.

Granting the preceding conditions, there is, however, no reason why a dictatorship cannot endure, or why the dictator, as age comes on, cannot select a successor to continue in a similar path. Furthermore, there is no requirement that the governments furnished by such dictatorships shall be of better than mediocre quality.

So, in political theory and experience, there are no reasons why the present Italian and Russian dictatorships may not endure, in practically their present forms, for one or several generations. If this should prove to be the case, each system might furnish its lessons and its special inspirations for the rest of the world. But neither system could furnish *the* lesson of a coherent and comprehensive political and economic system of an ultimately desirable type. The processes of political evolution are clearly and obviously, although by slow and painful processes, trending toward popular and representative forms of government, and we should be disregarding the plain evidence if we failed to think of the details of an ultimate economic system in terms other than those appropriate to a political background of the democratic type.

The proponents of the present Russian and Italian systems claim, however, that, in each case, the present government represents only a transitional stage toward an ultimate more popular form. The elements of these transitions, so far as an outside observer can determine, are, however, somewhat intangible.

In both countries the idea appears to be that, after a generation of education, the populations as a whole will be so thoroughly trained in the doctrines and practices of state capitalism and of Fascism, respectively, that truly popular governments may then be instituted, without resulting changes in the political and economic systems.

Our discussion of political liberties and of special political factors has, however, gone far enough. The essential point is that if general lessons for the future are to be taught by any, or all, of the politico-economic systems under examination, such lessons will be those that are appropriate to democratic forms of government. We may, therefore, eliminate from our further consideration the question of political forms and political liberties and may confine ourselves to those economic principles and those economic liberties and restraints that can have an enduring place in a democracy.

For these purely economic considerations, we may clear ground, in the beginning, by recognizing that in economics, as in all other realities, there are no absolute blacks and whites. We must deal always with infinite shades of gray and with infinite degrees of compromise. No one, today, will claim that a sound society should not, in one manner or another, protect all its members from destructive privation. The question is how far this protection should be carried in the direction of equality of economic reward, regardless of equality of productive effort. No one, furthermore, will claim that all economic powers should be reserved to the state, or that there should be no economic liberties permitted to the individual. The question is wholly of an effective and desirable balance between the two. And finally, no one will claim that we should not, if necessary, make some sacrifices, in economic efficiency or otherwise, to assure a greater stability of employment and a greater continuity of family incomes. Once more the question is at what point in the direction of complete stabilization the losses will begin to overbalance the gains.

In determining the ultimate working out of these several compromises in democratic society, we are face to face once more with the fact that our measure of values must be an evolutionary one, and that we are concerned with what will and can be under the play and counter-play of human instincts, rather than with what ought to be according to our own particular notions.

We can, however, find some guidance in the fact that evolution, in the long run, will not work contrary to the plain verities. So far, then, as we can determine absolute economic facts and laws, or can place our fingers upon dominating and ingrained human instincts, we are safe in asserting that economic systems that are concordant with such facts and instincts will have value and endure—while, in the reverse direction, systems that are discordant with such facts and instincts will, in due time, change or pass away.

Our first approach to a consideration of economic systems must rather obviously concern itself with the extent to which a normal society and normal human beings will wish to establish a complete or partial equalization of economic satisfactions among the able-bodied and able-minded, regardless of individual productivity. Against such equalization of rewards there appears to be a universal human instinct. The Russian Government, even though it may adhere in theory to the extreme socialistic doctrine "from each according to his ability, to each according to his need," has in practice introduced piece rates in its factories, and is adopting all the expedients of individualistic capitalism to secure increased production.

When this issue is squarely faced, in the case of obvious and tangible differences between the individual workers of any group, the answer is instinctive and automatic. The individual demands, as a matter of economic right, a reward that is in relative proportion to his effort. No productive system, other than one of pure slavery, has secured efficiency in output, up to date, without allowing such variations in rewards; and no executive of experience fails to recognize the prime importance of an accurate gradation of compensation in proportion to individual deserts. Faulty gradations, or the absence of gradations, may, and often do, have so depressing an effect on morale that the average production and the average possible wage may be lower than the minimum wage under a properly graded plan of compensation. The ancient curse of Adam still holds power, and no man yet has come to believe that he should sweat while others, equally able-bodied but less energetic or capable, enjoy in whole or in part the fruits of his labors.

If the present Russian government were to crys-

tallize and express its sentiments, it is doubtful
whether it would deny to any manual or brain
worker a full reward for his individual productivity,
however great that might be. There is, in fact, little
danger in direct demands for equalization of economic reward; the real danger is indirect and in-
sidious. It arises from the belief, or perhaps the
mere wish-thought, of the less competent elements
of society, that somewhere and somehow in the economic scheme of things there is a vast fund of un-
earned and ill-gotten wealth that may and should be
tapped, not to supply that insurance against absolutely destructive privation for which all civilized
societies recognize the need, but rather to relieve the
able-bodied individual from his normal obligations
to foresight and self-reliant provision for emergen-
cies and his old age.

The whole question of social insurance is once
again a question of compromise, and requires its
own separate consideration. For the moment, the
point to be made is that we may safely adopt, as one
of our major premises, the assumption that any ultimate economic system, to be concordant with basic
human instincts and with basic human experience,
must provide rewards in due proportion to individual productivity.

The tacit acceptance of the preceding premise by
the present Russian government has at one stroke
transformed its theory from that of communism to
that of state capitalism, but even in this latter respect the processes of compromise between state and
individual functions are in evidence. The development of agriculture by direct state agencies has attained, apparently, to 50 per cent of the total pro-

duction, and this process may go still further. On the other hand, it is stated that 40 per cent of industrial production is still turned out under handicraft methods by individuals, families, or associated groups of families.

So far as the rapidly changing picture in Russia permits any conclusions to be reached, it would appear that these handicraft workers may continue to constitute a permanent and substantial element in the productive forces of the country, and that the state organization of production will confine itself, in the main, to the key industries and those that lend themselves to large-scale factory operations.

However, even if large elements of the Russian economy retain more or less permanently their individualistic character, the development of the key industries, and the factory industries as a whole, by the state will constitute in itself an important and far-reaching variation from other economic systems. And it is rather obviously to this feature of the Russian system that we should address our main consideration.

Before beginning this special analysis we may, however, clear ground to advantage in several directions.

The prime factors in any economic system are labor (mental or manual), reproducible capital, and natural resources. The value of natural resources—land, forests, water power, and mineral deposits—may readily be absorbed by society in the form of annual rentals or depletion charges, without interfering with individual economic initiative, and perhaps with some advantage through the widening of the opportunities open to the individual. England is today imposing a general land tax, and Italy or the United States might readily do so without any essential changes in their economic systems. In the United States, actual or equivalent rents of natural resources account, roughly, for only 8 per cent of the national income, and this percentage may decline with the progress of agricultural changes, the stabilization of population, and the shifting of residential quarters from the congested centers into city suburbs under the influence of the automobile and other improved transportation. The problem is important, but not dominating; and, in any case, it is clearly separable from the other factors we are considering.

A similar separation is possible with respect to social insurance and to the stabilization of employment and family incomes. Social insurance is already highly, perhaps in some cases too highly, developed in countries that are operating under individualistic capitalism. When sanely and properly developed, it is a necessary and natural adjunct to such systems. The particular systems of social insurance that are developed in Italy or Russia, or in England, Germany, or the United States, may vary in character and in present and ultimate advantages or disadvantages, but they can be considered as a thing apart from the fundamental forms of economic structure.

An entirely similar situation exists, although perhaps less obviously, with respect to the stabilization of employment and family incomes.

At the moment when these lines were written, in

a locality over sixty miles from the nearest railroad station, I had just concluded an argument with a dusky gentleman as to whether or not he would work for me the following day. His preference was clearly for a day of leisure. While his fellow workers show slightly more interest in employment than they did before the recent depression, personal service still tends to be granted, in most cases, as a distinct favor to the employer.

This condition is typical of the differences that exist between highly organized and highly productive economic systems and those that are in their primitive stages. It would not be unfair to the Russian system to counter its claim for an absence of unemployment by saying that there is no unemployment in an organized army—but it is much more pertinent to point out that, with a national income estimated by the Soviet authorities at thirty-four billion rubles for a population of about one hundred and sixty millions, the per capita income in Russia is, at the best, only slightly over one hundred dollars per annum, as compared with incomes that are from two to seven or more times as great in other civilized countries.

If we make any allowance for the depreciation of the ruble in internal purchasing power, the per capita income in Russia may be less than $100. One competent estimate sets the figure at substantially less than one-tenth of the 1929 estimate of $734 per capita for the United States.

With respect to the stabilization of employment, such differences as the preceding cease to be those of degree and become differences of kind; and the

Russian system might progress successfully for a full generation before any lessons from its handling of the unemployment problem could be wholly pertinent to conditions as they now exist in the United States. However, as I shall attempt to show later, the problem of a reasonable stabilization of employment should not be insoluble even under the advanced individualistic economy of the United States, and may properly be treated as a question apart from that of fundamental economic structure.

The elements of our immediate inquiry now become simplified. We may assume that the lessons to be taught by the three systems under consideration must, in the end, be appropriate to essentially democratic political forms, and to a full development of political liberties. We may eliminate questions of foreign relations and of pure communism in the distribution of economic rewards. And we may further eliminate problems of the nationalization of the rents of land and natural resources, and of social insurance and the stabilization of employment, as being common to, and soluble under, all systems.

With these eliminations made, we reduce our problem to that of efficient and humanly acceptable balance between social and individual economic activities—to determining what compromise between social economic powers and individual economic liberties may most surely create that abiding conviction of the people as a whole in the usefulness and worthiness of their social order which, as has been said before, is the first essential to national unity. It is to this simplified inquiry that my next lecture will be addressed.

II. The Compromise between State and Individual Functions

In my previous lecture I narrowed our immediate inquiry regarding individualistic capitalism, Fascism, and Russian state capitalism to the old problem of the proper balance between social and individual ownership of capital and control of economic activities.

In approaching this central problem, it is essential that we should consider first the premises upon which our reasoning may be based. From the standpoint of the satisfaction of human instincts and the development of true national unity, individualistic capitalism either does or does not create, and must or need not continue to create, harmful disparities in wealth and individual income. Similarly, from the standpoint of pure efficiency in production, the system of individualistic capitalism either is more efficient, or has a greater tendency to improve in efficiency, than the system of state capitalism—or the reverse.

The major Marxian premise is that interest and dividends on reproducible capital tend to absorb all the increasing productivity of the capitalistic system (excluding that absorbed by rents of natural resources) and to leave to labor only a subsistence wage.

The major premise of individualistic capitalism is that capital (excluding land and natural resources) receives in the long run only a living wage, and that the increased productivity of an advancing economic system accrues in major part to labor in the form of increased real wages.

It is obvious that both premises cannot be correct, and it is of primary importance to determine the facts.

According to the usual economic theory, the normal interest rate is determined by the reward that is necessary to induce men to abstain in adequate amount from purchases of consumption goods, in order that, by investing their money at interest, they may provide the funds necessary for the output of those producers' goods which are required to satisfy the demand for new capital. Economic theory also indicates that, where free competition exists, the operations of such competition should give to the individual capitalistic producer only a temporary reward for each addition of new and improved machinery, over and above compensation for risk and a normal rate of interest on the added investment. In the long run, therefore, any balance of increased productivity, above that required to maintain the current rate of return on the added capital, should accrue to labor, either in reduced prices, or in increased wages, or in a combination of the two.

To test the soundness of the preceding theory it is necessary to know first of all whether the capitalistic system, in its present form, operates substantially as a competitive system, or is largely characterized by monopoly operations of such sort as to secure substantially more than a normal return on invested capital.

If it proves to be true that the modern capitalistic system operates substantially on a competitive basis, it is necessary, next, to determine whether this system does operate, in fact, to increase real wages in general accordance with increases in productivity, as the theory indicates that it should.

In the United States, where individualistic capitalism has perhaps reached its outstanding development, we are fortunate in having, during recent years, many sources of tested and reliable statistical information bearing upon these questions.

The records of the Interstate Commerce Commission and of the state public service commissions supply adequate evidence that our great public services—the railroads, the telephones and telegraphs, and the power and light companies—are genuinely regulated, and, on the average, earn little if any more than is necessary to attract the new capital required for their growth and expansion. Questions of rates and charges are argued from time to time furiously and at length, but the net result in the end, in spite of popular and political furor and excitement, is usually to reduce the issue to that of increasing or decreasing the allowed return on investment by fractions, rather than by whole units, of 1 per cent. We may, therefore, reasonably assume that the great regulated monopolies in the United States are receiving little, if any, more than a living wage for their capital.

If we turn next to the production of commodities, we have, first of all, a general but very adequate knowledge that the vast bulk of the commodities that we consume are produced and distributed under conditions of very active competition. Food, clothing and house furnishings fall strictly into this category.

There remain, in general, in the category of possible monopolies, only such commodities as steel and the non-ferrous metals, cement, lumber, machine tools, etc. As to these articles, the ordinary consumer has less tangible and direct evidence of active competition, and the suspicion more often arises that monopoly exactions may be prevalent. For this reason it is appropriate to examine somewhat more closely the evidence as to the presence or absence of monopoly exactions in productive operations.

Our first evidence lies in the existence of the Sherman and Clayton acts and of the Federal Trade Commission—plus our knowledge of the credit that would accrue to any ambitious politician who might successfully launch an attack upon an outstanding and illegal monopoly. Large-scale business operations are conducted in full view of the Federal Government, from many and varied angles. There is adequate evidence that the antitrust laws are honestly, and even sometimes too vigorously, enforced. And the reasonable presumption is that no serious large-scale monopoly exactions can exist without promptly being called to the attention of the governmental authorities.

As a further indication of the effective governmental control of monopolies in the United States, we have the reverse movement of various trade associations to work out with the Federal authorities a basis for minimizing the harmful effects of excessive competition.

Supplementing this general evidence as to the absence of monopoly exactions, we have more specific evidence in the corporation income tax returns, which are compiled in totals by industrial and other significant groups. The particularly significant figure that can be derived from these compilations is the percentage of gross sales available, as net profit, for interest and dividends on invested capital. During the period from 1918 to 1928, inclusive, this percentage for all manufacturing corporations varied roughly from .3 per cent to 7.3 per cent in different years, with an average of about 6.04 per cent. Similar figures made up from individual corporation reports for a selected list of the more successful industrial companies, during the period from 1920 to 1929, inclusive, show a range of average profit margins, for different years, varying from 5.0 per cent to 14.4 per cent, with a general average for the period of 9.4 per cent.

The preceding figures give no indication of excessive monopoly profits. It will be noted, furthermore, that they involve no question as to the actual investment in industrial operations. Their accuracy is dependent solely on the correctness of the figures for gross sales and the accuracy of the governmental audits for income tax purposes—and it would be possible to present much fervent testimony as to the latter to prove that the income tax authorities are overlooking few opportunities to collect their full dues.

Still further very definite evidence as to absence of abnormal monopoly profits is found in the continuing studies that are made of the financial and operating results of all important corporations by the research staffs of a multitude of investment organizations. Contrary to what might be the expectation, these studies are not made for the purpose of searching out and investing in monopolies, but for the purpose of avoiding investments where abnormal rates or profit are dependent upon monopoly situations of the kinds that experience has shown will sooner or later break down with disastrous results to the industry as a whole. Investments in monopolies are looked upon with favor by investment experts only in those instances where it is clear that monopoly power is being used to assure stability of reasonable returns, rather than to obtain excessive profits.

Combining all the preceding evidence, I shall venture the assertion that, in the United States today and during recent years, the total of monopoly profits in large-scale operations, measured as the excess of such profits over normal competitive profits, is distinctly under one per cent, and probably under one-half of one per cent, of the national income. If this be true, we are justified in believing that the system of individualistic capitalism in the United States operates substantially, and in effect, on a competitive basis—and I should expect to find that, with minor degrees of difference, the individualistic capitalism of other countries operates in the same way.

If, then, we assume a competitive capitalism, the next question is to what extent such a system operates in practice according to economic theory. Do the returns on invested capital tend to absorb a constant or decreasing percentage of the total product, with accompanying increases in real wages; or is the tendency toward increasing percentages of return to capital and a fixed or declining rate of real wages?

As to the rate of return on invested capital, satisfactory statistics in the United States have been available only since the establishment of the Fed-

eral corporation income tax; and the indications
from these figures are somewhat less significant
than they might otherwise be, by reason of the abnormal conditions that existed during the war and
immediate post-war period. However, the figures
for the year 1926 may be taken as typical of a recent normally prosperous year, without an extreme
inflation of activity. For that year, the total assets
of manufacturing corporations were reported to be
about $65,000,000,000, from which should, however,
be deducted about $5,000,000,000 to adjust current
assets to net figures, making the adjusted total
about $60,000,000,000. On this total of assets, the
net profits, after Federal and other taxes had been
deducted, amounted to about 6.7 per cent, or $4,000,-
000,000, available for interest and dividends. Owing
to the ownership of many companies, in whole or in
part, by other corporations, the income tax figures
include certain duplications of assets and earnings.
The elimination of such duplications should not,
however, appreciably affect the 6.7 per cent return
just calculated, but would reduce the total money
employed in manufacturing, in 1926, to, perhaps,
$50,000,000,000.

As compared with the preceding figure of 6.7 per
cent for earnings, the income tax statistics indicate
that actual disbursements on account of dividends
and net interest payments, during 1926, were at the
rate of about 5.6 per cent.

For a further check on the rate of earnings on invested capital, it is of interest to apply the usual
ratio of capital turnover to the 6.04 per cent average
rate of profit on gross sales mentioned some time
previously. For the period 1913 to 1921, inclusive,

the average rate of turnover in manufacturing operations[1] appears to have been about 86 per cent—that is to say, gross sales, in an average year, were equal to 86 per cent of the total money used by manufacturing corporations. On this basis, the average net profit available for interest and dividends should be at the rate of 5.2 per cent, which agrees as closely as could be expected with the previous figure of 6.7 per cent for the prosperous year of 1926.

For a long term comparison with the preceding figures, we may revert to the frequently quoted statement by Adam Smith, that, in his time (prior to 1776), double interest was considered a fair profit. That chapter of the *Wealth of Nations* which deals with the profits of invested capital, or of "stock" as Adam Smith calls it, might be written almost without change today. Double interest is the "fair and reasonable profit" to which the successful merchant or manufacturer aspires. Single interest is more often the profit he obtains. And a loss of both principal and interest is the frequent penalty for failure.

The evidence is clear, even if scattered and fragmentary, that the average of all capital invested in trade and industry in the United States earns, in the long run, only a very moderate premium for risk, above bond interest—and there are many who have studied the question most closely who doubt whether any net premium at all could be shown, if full account were taken of the recurring losses in legitimate but unsuccessful ventures.

This conclusion brings us one step further ahead

[1] See Bliss, *Financial and Operating Ratios in Management*, p. 307.

in our analysis. Capitalism in the United States appears, on the whole, to be truly competitive. Competition seems to hold the returns on invested capital to an average that represents only a very moderate premium, if any, over bond interest. Labor should be the "residuary legatee," as economic theory would indicate. What, once again, are the facts? Is labor receiving a constant or increasing share in the product of industry? Are real wages increasing? And, finally, is it possible, as might be the case, that real wages are increasing, in spite of the fact that capital is absorbing an increasing share of the product?

With respect to the first of the preceding questions, the most significant and reliable figures are probably those of the National Bureau of Economic Research, which, in its first investigation into the distribution of the national income for the period from 1909 to 1918 inclusive, found the division of the combined net value product of mines, factories, and land transportation, between earnings of employees and returns for management and the use of property, to range from 68.7 per cent to wages and salaries and 31.3 per cent to management and capital in 1909, up to a high point of 77.3 per cent to salaries and wages and 22.7 per cent to management and capital in 1918, with an intermediate low point of 66.7 per cent to wages and salaries in 1916.

A later study by the Bureau carries similar figures forward through the year 1925, and gives the percentage that the payments received by employees in the form of wages, salaries, and pensions, constituted of the entire realized income drawn by individuals from the three major industrial groups.

For manufacturing, these percentages ranged from 79.9 per cent in 1909, to a high point of 87.8 per cent in 1925, with an intermediate low point of 76.8 per cent in 1916.

For mines, quarries, and oil wells, the similar percentages ranged from 71.4 per cent in 1909, through a low point of 60.5 per cent in 1916, to a high point of 78.5 per cent in 1920, and then declined to 71.8 per cent in 1925.

The corresponding figures for transportation, communication, and electric power, ranged from a low point of 63.9 per cent in 1909, to a high point of 82.7 per cent in 1920, and then declined to 75.6 per cent in 1925.

As to all the preceding figures, it should be noted that they relate to highly organized industries, in which the compensation of management is included, in the main, under the heading of salaries and wages. For such industries, the distribution indicated may be taken, without sensible error, to be the distribution between capital and labor. When, however, we take the extreme case in the other direction—that of agriculture—we find, on the average, that less than 15 per cent of the entire realized income is paid out in salaries and wages. The balance of 85 per cent is, however, mainly compensation for the work of the farmer and his family, rather than return for the use of the farmer's capital.

As an independent check on these figures, we have Professor Douglas' *Study of Real Wages in the United States from 1890 to 1926,* in which he concludes:

If we take the material (relating to manufactures) as a whole, therefore, and consider the value product of industry and not merely the physical products, it seems impossible to conclude that the share of labor has decreased during the quarter century from 1899 to 1925. The evidence indicates, instead, that labor's share increased from 1899 to 1921, and that, while it has decreased since then, it was in 1925 still above the average of 1899.

For my own personal purposes, I reviewed, some years ago, all the available evidence as to the distribution of the national income of the United States and reached the conclusion that, of this total, 68 per cent was received directly or indirectly as returns for personal service, 24 per cent as returns for the use of reproducible capital (including actual or equivalent interest on the value of residential structures), and 8 per cent as actual or equivalent rent of land and natural resources.

I have no reason to believe that these percentages have changed substantially during the ten years that have elapsed since the original estimates were made. My impression—although it is only an impression—is, however, that the long term trend is toward a slow increase in the percentage accruing to labor and personal service.

In my previous lecture I gave some reasons for believing that the percentage accruing as rents of natural resources might decline. There would also seem to be some possibility of a decline in the percentage accruing to capital. The new science of business management is concentrating its efforts very definitely in the direction of increasing the annual volume of business and annual value of production per dollar of invested capital. Chain store operations have certainly been effective in this respect. If the rates of return on industrial and commercial

capital continue to maintain that fixed relation to
interest rates that they apparently have maintained
for over one hundred and fifty years, since the days
of Adam Smith, each increase in the volume of business done, per dollar of invested capital, must, in
due time, result in an increase not only in real
wages but in the percentage of the national income
that accrues to labor and personal service.

Cyclical variations in prices, in interest rates,
and in business activity, may obscure this trend—
but in due time we may have convincing statistical
evidence that it exists. If we were to be guided
wholly by the figures of the National Bureau of Economic Research, previously quoted, we might, indeed, assume a rapid increase in the percentage of
the product of industry that accrues to labor. But
my impression is that much of this apparent increase was due to war conditions and to cyclical
movements, and that the actual trend is at a very
much slower rate.

As opposed to the possibility of labor receiving an
increasing share in the product of industry, it is of
interest to note, in the reverse direction, that there
is nothing in economic theory to prevent a large and
continuing increase in the percentage of the product
that accrues to capital. New equipment might continue to be introduced in manufacturing plants just
so long as each addition would return any small
margin above, say, 6 per cent on the investment.
Under these circumstances the capital investment
per employee might mount to very high figures, and
the proportion of the product accruing to capital
might steadily rise. In actual practice, however, new
and improved machinery is not installed on the

basis of a potential 6 per cent return, but rather with the expectation that the machine will return its original cost, in improved efficiency, within a two to five-year period. The prevalence of this practice was shown by an inquiry made in connection with the report of the Committee on Recent Economic Changes, of the President's Conference on Unemployment, which showed that, out of two hundred manufacturing companies replying to the inquiry, 43.6 per cent required that new equipment should return its cost, through savings, in a period of two years or less, and 64.1 per cent required that such equipment should pay for itself in three years or less. It is this fact, that the increasing mechanization of industry is on a basis providing a very great margin over and above ordinary interest charges, which explains the continuing high share of labor in the total product, and may make possible further increases in such share.

We have come now to the final step in the analysis of the economic relations between capital and labor under competitive capitalism. It is unnecessary to repeat the evidence as to the rate of increase of physical production in the United States. Estimates vary slightly, but agree, for all practical purposes, that such increase has been for an extended period at a rate somewhat over, rather than under, 3 per cent per annum, as compared with an annual increase of about 1½ per cent in population. No one, furthermore, who has any measure of the suppressed energies that are awaiting only the passing of the present depression to reassert themselves, can doubt that we shall very shortly see a resumption of substantially this same economic advance.

The question is, however, whether this increased productivity has been tangibly evidenced by increases in real wages.

If we study periods that are long enough, there can be no question as to the answer. Real wages in the United States have much more than doubled since 1865. The trend becomes confused only as we deal in short periods, when it may be obscured by cyclical movements in business, by violent changes in prices and money rates, by rapid increases in taxes and governmental expenditures, and by many other factors that smooth themselves out in the longer view.

The recent and immediate pre-war period in the United States has been a particularly difficult one from the preceding viewpoint. An extremely rapid expansion and mechanization of industry has been combined with violent economic changes of many kinds, due to the war and the war's aftermath.

Under these circumstances, we are fortunate in having Professor Douglas' careful study of real wages in the United States from 1890 to 1926. His most significant conclusion may, I believe, be given in his own words by saying that "In 1926 the average hourly money earnings of some 14 million workers were 233 per cent above that of the nineties, and 125 per cent above the 1914 average. This was equivalent to an increase in purchasing power of 38 and 30 per cent respectively."

My own figures made some years ago indicated that real hourly wages, largely owing to the extreme depression in commodity prices, were substantially above their normal trend line during the ten-year period of the nineties. The normal trend line was, however, reëstablished from 1900 to 1914, and the comparisons with 1914 figures, made by Professor Douglas, should not, therefore, be misleading. However, my further impression is that a continuation of the normal trend line from 1914 to 1926 would have shown an increase of only about one-half the 30 per cent increase in real hourly wages found by Professor Douglas during this same period. Whether Professor Douglas' figures indicate a more rapid up trend in real wages than before the war, or simply a temporarily high level of such wages in 1926, can, perhaps, be determined only after approximately normal conditions have been reëstablished with the passing of the present depression. The important point for our present purpose, in any case, is the evidence of a continuing long term increase in real wages, which is quite concordant with the economic facts and theory we have previously considered.

Taking all the preceding statistics and studies together, the system of individualistic capitalism, as exemplified most conspicuously in the United States, may reasonably be held to have certain definite characteristics. It is fundamentally, and in practice, a competitive system. It increases in total productivity at the rate of about 3 per cent per annum, and in per capita productivity at a rate between 1 per cent and 2 per cent per annum. It increases real wages, in the long run, at a rate concordant with the increases in per capita production. Its total production is distributed in the proportions of about 68 per cent to labor and personal services, 24 per cent as returns on reproducible capital, and 8 per cent as rents of land natural resources. Labor and capital share in its industrial production in the ratio of about 70 per cent to labor and 30 per cent to capital; and, so far as the limited evidence may be trusted, the share of labor is tending to increase rather than to decrease.

To the preceding we may add certain other significant items.

The realized national income[2] of the people of the United States in 1926 was about $80,000,000,000, or $700 per capita, a figure that is nearly double that of other advanced industrial nations, and perhaps ten times that of Russia. Large salaries and professional earnings are a negligible element in the distribution of the national income, the larger individual incomes being derived almost wholly from interest, dividends, rents, etc. The total of cash dividends disbursed and net interest payments made by corporations, during the normally prosperous year of 1926, was about $6,200,000,000. If we eliminate inter-company payments, the net payments to individuals were perhaps something over $5,000,000,000, which figure checks satisfactorily with the total of $4,900,000 reported as roughly similar income on individual income tax returns for that year. The total of all individual incomes in excess of $10,000 per individual for 1926 was $7,530,000,000, of which amount about $2,000,000,000 was, however, represented by the questionably real item of capital gains.

For comparison with the preceding figures, we have the estimate of the Department of Commerce that the requirements for new capital in the United States average about $10,000,000,000 per annum.

[2] *National Income and Its Purchasing Power,* last column, p. 74.

This confirms, for the United States, the fact recognized by many socialistic writers, and evident in the present operations of the Russian Government, that neither the socialization of large-scale industry nor the direct confiscation of large incomes would in themselves permit an improvement in standards of living, but would, on the contrary, probably throw upon the government definite obligations for new capital that would be in excess of any amounts so realized.

As opposed to the preceding picture for the advanced individualistic capitalism of the United States, we have in Russia an experiment in state capitalism that begins with a nation in a primitive stage of economic development and with a per capita national income that is from one-seventh to one-tenth of that which we enjoy.

The fallacy of the major Marxian premise, upon which the Russian developments are based, may be demonstrated to anyone who is not intellectually or psychopathically unable to examine and face the facts.

The further fallacy that state capitalism cannot succeed in a single nation without a world revolution against individualistic capitalism is, we may hope, in process of sincere abandonment by the Russian Government. If persisted in, it would involve the equivalent of a Mohammedan holy war by Russia against the majority of civilized nations—and such nations would be fully justified not only in the passive opposition involved in non-recognition, but in the use of any other measures necessary to oppose effectively that communistic propaganda abroad which, until very recently at least, has been backed and supported, directly or indirectly, by the Russian Government.

Every population and every civilization has its considerable percentage of those who cannot, or do not, adapt themselves to the restraint of their environment. A few are purely psychopathic cases. A larger group are intellectuals—college professors and others—who have not acquired philosophic adjustment to the fact that the world must be run, on the whole, by super-energetic, self-satisfied mediocrities, plus a sprinkling of monomaniacs, on a basis of wholly realistic morals. But the largest group of all includes those who, to all intents and purposes, are stone-age men living in the age of electricity.

For one nation to tell the stone-age men of another that they have a religious obligation to indulge in their natural instincts for pillage and murder is an international crime of the first order—and it is fortunate for the peace of the world that some perception of this fact seems at last to be dawning upon the Russian authorities.

However, there is no teacher like responsibility, and the fact that the present Soviet Government has endured for some years, and may continue to endure, is the best guaranty that it will "accept the universe" and not quarrel eternally with the verities. It would be idle to attempt to forecast the ultimate course of Russian events. Nevertheless, the Russian people will certainly survive—and by evolution or revolution they will in due time develop a settled political and economic order.

In this development we may see paralleled, for the social and economic field, that rapid evolution— if we measure in terms of evolutionary time—that characterized the development of modern representative government from its beginnings in the feudal system. Not only politics and economics, but religion and the family relations, have been cast into the Russian smelter. We are fortunate that we do not have to pay the price of the smelting, but we may learn lessons in social metallurgy when the run-off comes.

I must confess, however, to being an incurable optimist where the United States is concerned. The Russian experiment starts from a point too far down on the economic scale to have any controlling present or early future significance for ourselves, or for any other nations that approach our level of economic development. Furthermore, I have the firm conviction that, long before Russia attains to an enduring stability of social order, we here in the United States, without sacrificing the values of individual initiative and of individual economic liberties, shall have far outstripped the Russia of that ultimate date in effective measures of social progress.

For the preceding reasons, we shall, I believe, find it much more profitable to consider the natural steps that we may take in the development of our own social economy, rather than to look too hopefully toward any lessons that the Russian experiment may teach.

The elimination of the Marxian fallacy reduces the argument for state capitalism very largely to that of increased economic efficiency, with more recent emphasis upon claims for superior effectiveness in industrial planning and in the stabilization of employment. To these claims must be added the supposed advantages to be derived from a greater equalization of wealth and income, unaccompanied by any directly resulting rise in general standards of living.

The superior efficiency of state operation of industries is, however, purely hypothetical. There is a convincing amount of unbiased testimony to show that the government-operated railroads, communication systems and public utilities of other countries rarely, if ever, attain to the measure of efficiency in operation, or of true effectiveness in public service, that have been attained by our own private systems under governmental regulation. A public service, or perhaps even an industry, may occasionally and temporarily be stepped up to a new level of efficiency by government control, but this early gain is apt soon to be lost through that failure to make subsequent progress which seems to be the inevitable result of political and bureaucratic management.

This vital difference between immediate gains in efficiency and those ultimate gains which result from the free play of individual initiative is often overlooked. There is no measure of immediate gain in economic efficiency that could compensate us for the loss of even a small portion of that one to two per cent annual increase in per capita production which is almost wholly the product of our own unfettered individual initiative.

It would, however, be carrying this argument to the extreme to contend that there should be no new fields opened to the employment of public capital, or that our choice of administrative agencies for important economic activities must be absolutely limited to the governmental departments, and the private corporations, regulated or otherwise, with which we are now familiar.

As indicated in my previous lecture, we can, if we wish, readily socialize the great values represented by land and natural resources, by the simple device of absorbing rental and depletion charges through taxation.

In recent years we have also taken a very important step in the creation of new social capital by the building of an immense transportation system in the form of improved automobile highways. And a significant move along somewhat different lines has been the creation of the Port of New York Authority by the joint action of the states of New York and New Jersey, which authority is operating as a purely public agency in the employment of private capital to supply improved transportation facilities on a commercially self-sustaining basis.

If we wished to go a step further than the preceding we might also do so, without any vital changes in our present system, by permitting our governmental units to invest in the bondable values of our great public services. In such case, the bond interest received by the government might preferably be employed to reduce taxation, but could if desired be remitted to the public in the form of reduced rates and charges.

I am not necessarily advocating any of the preceding plans, but am mentioning them simply to show some of the ways in which the social capital might be increased, and has in some cases actually been increased, without fundamental changes in our economic structure, and while still leaving a broad field open to the play and development of individual initiative. The essential point is that we have neither in our political nor in our economic system any fixed barriers against whatever development of social capital and social activities may be justified by experience. Furthermore, if the genius for compromise that we have inherited with our political traditions holds true, we must inevitably progress steadily, in the future as in the past, toward that social responsiveness in our economic organization, which is vastly more important than any particular line of division between state and individual capital.

On other occasions, when discussing this same subject, I have referred to the fact that it is a mistake to assume that there must be a sharp dividing line between the economic activities of the state and those that are purely individual. Such sharp division is entirely theoretical. The normal economic organism, like the bodily organism, is essentially ganglionic in its nervous controls. The central political brain, like the central human brain, is unfitted for, and cannot be burdened with, routine control of the vital functions. Such control must be exercised by separate ganglia, each duly adapted to its special function.

So in our own economic development, the railroads and great communication systems have already become very completely socialized under ganglionic controls that are very largely free from political interference, and are represented by the joint activities of their own managements and the public regulating authorities.

This development of our public services, supplemented perhaps by the creation of special agencies like the Port of New York Authority, represents a very significant trend—the type of slow and patient compromise from which, in the end, the greatest of social values always arise.

The substance of this development lies in the effective responsiveness of the economic agencies to public needs. The forms of control and management are less important. They may, and probably should, vary through a wide range, according to the special conditions involved in each case. And finally the question of the ownership of the capital involved is the least important of all, and may well be left to its own gradual solution, which once again will probably be by compromise.

In this picture of the gradual working out of new social agencies I am in close agreement with some thoughtful socialists who realize the impossibility of an effective administration of economic activities under control that is not fully divorced from the ordinary and necessary run of political activities— and I should differ with such socialists only as to the urgency and extent of further socialization, and as to the importance of preserving individual economic initiative.

If, now, we leave the question of the socialization of economic activities to the gradual working out previously indicated and turn to the question of the undesirability of large incomes and large wealth, in themselves, we are touching upon a problem that I shall attempt to solve only by asking the question whether or not all problems must be solved by political action, or whether there do not remain a few that may be left for handling by the private and community conscience?

We have, I believe, attempted a premature transfer of some elements of the liquor question from the courts of public opinion to those of law—and it may be quite possible to make the same mistake in attempts to penalize wealth by law merely because it *is* wealth. It is quite certain, in any case, that our income and other taxes affecting wealth have failed very largely to operate according to their theoretical intent. Any experienced accountant will testify that corporation income taxes operate almost wholly to increase the cost of commodities and services. It is not, however, so generally recognized that there is an apparent tendency for personal income taxes to be similarly shifted, by reason of increasing differentials between the rates of return on tax exempt bonds and those that are taxable. This differential carries through to dividends by reason of the fact that dividends tend to maintain a direct relation to the return on taxable, rather than tax exempt, bonds.

The theory of taxation has been bluntly stated to be that of "obtaining the greatest volume of feathers with the fewest squawks." In the language of the tax experts, this statement is more politely translated into that of "assessing taxation according to ability to pay"—and what seem rather specious attempts have been made to build up a moral justification for this doctrine of convenience.

There can be no question as to the desirability of efforts to prevent the dishonest acquisition of wealth—and we may justify inheritance taxes on amounts in excess of those necessary to provide a very moderate degree of security for descendants and dependents, on the assumption that such taxes will tend to develop the initiative of successive generations. But to assess taxes on honestly acquired wealth, simply because it provides easy feather plucking for the tax gatherer, can, to my mind, end only in the degradation of the economic conscience of the public, besides very frequently failing to attain its avowed purpose and leading to exceedingly harmful economic strains and distortions.

As a pure incident to this question of great wealth, my own observations have convinced me that such wealth is very rarely acquired at the expense of labor or of consumers, as such. When we wish honey, we do not catch and strip each honeybee on its return from a day's work, but wait, instead, until the honey has been deposited in the comb. Similarly the acquisition of great wealth, when not purely accidental, appears usually to be the result of struggle and play and counter-play between the capitalists, large and small, that have already made their accumulations.

To touch now upon our final point with respect to possible economic developments in this country, we have the absorbing question of economic planning and the stabilization of employment. Our problem in economic planning is not, however, one of willingness to plan or of freedom to plan, but purely that of knowing how to plan. Capital has no desire to lend itself to the wasteful inflation of any industry, nor, on the other hand, will it hesitate to support the expansion of any activity that deserves and needs to grow. The Department of Commerce has already done much excellent work in economic planning and, particularly, in the elimination of waste through the simplification and standardization of products by conferences among producers. It should have no difficulty in carrying these steps to the practical limit of their possibilities. Furthermore, it would be difficult to surpass the economic planning that is done even today, by organizations such as our telephone and telegraph systems, and our automotive industry.

As a matter of fact, the whole basis of the competitive system is that of planning for the future, and it is a pure abstraction of theory to assume that a governmental planning bureau would make fewer or less serious mistakes than the competitive system does under the spur of its own self-interest. It is a very simple matter to plan the initial steps in a country's industrialization, as compared with the refinements of knowledge and calculation that are required to hold a highly developed economy in balance.

Economic planning is, in any case, a problem somewhat apart from that of maintaining an even and normal activity in the economic organization. It is probable that the present world-wide depression will not soon repeat itself with equal intensity. As the days pass, we can see more clearly that the present crisis is a definite aftermath of the Great War. Nevertheless, it is evident, particularly in the United States, that our constantly increasing productivity of articles of luxury and semi-luxury consumption is developing a sensitiveness in our economic operations that has not yet been counterbalanced by our efforts to attain stability. The problem is of dominating economic importance—it is of absolutely vital importance from the personal and human standpoint.

As I have indicated before, and as the best students of the subject have concluded, the question of economic crises is one which develops in importance with each advance in economic organization from its primitive agricultural stages to that of the highly developed industrial civilization. A civilization made up of absolutely self-contained agricultural and handicraft family units might have droughts—but it could have no unemployment. The Russian economic system is still too near this primitive economic stage to make its unemployment problems serious or its handling of them of real interest to countries with a high degree of industrial development.

With relation to the existing unemployment situation in the United States, the outstanding fact is the absolute unanimity of opinion as to the necessity for taking some action which shall at least tend to minimize, if not wholly to eliminate, such recurring cycles.

If I may attempt to express the consensus of opinion among those who are closest to the question and have studied it most carefully, there is substantial agreement regarding at least two vital points in any genuine program for employment stabilization.

The first agreement is that there is no single royal road to a solution of the problem, but that it must be handled separately by each industry, with the widest possible latitude allowed for trial and experimentation. To this end the manufacturers of the country have very reasonably indicated their desire that, regardless of any later action that may be taken with respect to state insurance plans, the private insurance companies should be permitted to write whatever policies may be necessary to make it possible for individual industrial units to test out such plans as may appear promising.

The second plan of agreement is that public funds should not be used for purposes of employment stabilization, but that the cost of such stabilization should be borne by the industries and employees involved, with the full expectation that the amounts appropriated by the various industries may in large part, if not wholly, be reflected in higher prices for their products.

To the above general principles I would add only my own first suggestion that compulsory savings plans, under which each employee would set aside, say, 5 per cent of his wages each month for his own unemployment reserve, might very properly be combined with the stabilization reserve plans of the various industries.

I suspect that these reserve funds, whether of industries or of individual employees, must be deposited under special arrangements whereby the Federal Government may facilitate the meeting of heavy drafts upon such accounts, without interference with normal credit operations and a possible contraction of general purchasing power at the very time when stability was the first requisite.

As a further suggestion, I would very tentatively propose that encouragement might be given to industrial stabilization by permitting the industries to take certain credits against Federal income taxes for appropriations made to stabilization reserves of any one of a variety of approved types. And, lest I appear to add to the troubles of an already harassed Treasury, I would suggest that the normal corporation income tax might be increased by the amount necessary to offset such credits.

It is too much to hope that variations in employment and business activity can ever be wholly eliminated. It may be treason to say it, but business depressions frequently pay their deferred dividends in economic sanity and in renewed economic efficiency. However, the price we are paying today is much too heavy for any remote benefits, and there cannot be the slightest doubt that the single most important economic and social problem before us is that of joining a reasonable security of employment and of family incomes to the increasing productivity and increasing real wages that our economic system has already fully demonstrated its ability to provide.

As indicated before, there seems to be no single royal road to the end we seek. Nevertheless, a long step forward toward employment stabilization should be possible if we can only forego cure-alls and extreme plans, and be satisfied to capitalize promptly the present unanimity of industry in favor of some definite, although conservative, approach to a solution of the problem. Stabilization reserves in industry, automatic savings plans for employees, reasonable preferences in employment according to length of service and family responsibilities, a moderate spreading of available employment during periods of depression, and a proper organization of public employment bureaus—all these represent constructively conservative first steps that we can take without risk of making major economic mistakes.

Furthermore, if we add to the preceding a reasonable regulation of public works, and such action on the part of the Federal Reserve System as may be justified by sound banking principles to check those prior inflations which are the breeders of depressions—with all these we may, I believe, reasonably hope that our next depression will show that real results have been accomplished and that our further task is only the refinement and polishing of the work already begun.

All these plans relate, of course, to the future. They cannot be effective to meet the present emergency, which must be and, I am certain, will be met by the combined agencies of private and public relief.

Attention to such direct relief should not, however, lead us to shirk another measure of immediate importance.

During the depression of 1921, I was called upon to advise certain companies as to their policy with respect to wage reductions. At that time I stated that conditions did not justify a decrease in wage rates—but, if I were called upon today to give similar advice, my answer would be different.

In the end, labor profits only when capital profits; and labor can afford, even less than capital, to risk that blighting effect upon business recovery that will result from attempts to maintain wage rates that begin to appear hopelessly out of line with the new levels of prices. It may be that, in due time, prices will return to something approaching their 1929 levels, but the current decline has been too great and too fundamental, and the prospects of recovery are too remote, to justify the wage policy that was appropriate in 1921.

Wage reductions must take place. Many reductions have, in fact, already taken place. The only question is as to the proper measure of such decreases. These should not exceed the decline in the cost of living. It may be that reductions of lesser amount will be effective. Furthermore, it may be appropriate that wage reductions shall be accompanied by pledges to restore the old scales *pro rata* with advances in the cost of living.

These are details that must be decided. The important point is, however, for the leaders of labor to show their statesmanship in meeting the plain necessities of the situation, and to prove that their care for their followers does not run to the point of demanding economic impossibilities. There is no reason to believe that temporary wage reductions will become permanent. Recovery of business activity will drag up wage rates in line with price recoveries generally—and labor leaders and public opinion in the United States are amply powerful to see to it that there is no undue lag in this process.

WORLD ECONOMIC PLANNING

BY NEWTON D. BAKER

WORLD ECONOMIC PLANNING

THE world has progressed a long way since 1918 in the liquidation of the consequences of the World War. To the popular mind, driven alternately by impatient hope and brooding anxiety, the results actually achieved may seem disappointing, but from a detached point of view, they are in fact fundamental in character and both more salutary and more far-reaching in effect than would have been deemed possible by the most optimistic observer at the conclusion of the war. Even the Treaty of Versailles, with what are now recognized as its plain imperfections and concessions to war passions, is coming to be regarded as containing a good starting place for future progress. By its direct and indirect effects, it has stimulated the discussions and established the agencies through which much of the progress made since 1918 has been rendered possible. It is difficult to reconstruct in our memories the atmosphere in which the Versailles Treaty was made. With the more obvious embarrassments of the situation I have here no concern. There were, of course, victors and vanquished, griefs and hatreds, greeds and aspirations, and responsible statesmen were called upon to reconstruct the international social order upon presumptions as to the economic and political consequences of their actions, and very much in the dark, indeed, as to the extent of the catastrophe which they were seeking to repair. The armistice operated only upon military operations—it did nothing to stay intellectual and emotional hostilities—and the representatives of peoples suddenly relieved from a great fear, and still suffering from a great agony, could do little more than apply first aid to a critically injured world. Hurried but fairly accurate estimates were made of the loss of life and destruction of property. Some account was taken of the possible effect of attempting longer to restrain racial aspirations which, under the old *régime,* had been contained, with difficulty, by force. But no thoughtful person at Versailles could have believed that a treaty written at such a time and under such circumstances could be a permanent, unchanging, and inelastic reordering of the institutions and aspirations of all mankind. That so much was able to be gotten into the treaty, by way of seed for future growth, is its great excellence, and it is juster to judge it by the things which have grown out of it, rather than by the things which remain in it to be outgrown. It was the general understanding at Versailles that the relations and obligations fixed by the treaty would, from time to time, be changed. President Wilson expressed this idea repeatedly while the treaty was under discussion, and after its signature he constantly pointed out the League of Nations, created by it, as the agency through which necessary changes were to be studied and the reconciliation of world opinion obtained. General Smuts perhaps phrased this general expectation more happily, and with more perfect foresight, than anybody else, when he said, ''I feel that in the Treaty we have not yet achieved the real peace to which our peoples were looking, but the real peace of the peoples ought to follow, complete, and amend the peace of the statesmen.''

It is in this clear recognition of the limitations

upon the power and possibilities of statesmen, and the duty and power of "the peoples," that I find the theme which I venture to discuss.

In a general way it may be said that the statesmen who have been busy about the post-war reconstruction have done well—far better than the world had any right to expect. They approached their task burdened with the traditions of the old diplomatic method and the traditional diplomatic point of view. A brilliant young American historical scholar recently has said that the diplomacy of the world immediately preceding our Spanish War was conducted "in a peculiarly felonious atmosphere." By 1914 there had been no improvement in this regard and the resumption of international relations, interrupted by the war, did not at once change for the better either the manners or the objectives of national policies. In the beginning, the League of Nations was a mere balloon sent up to discover whether there was substance enough in the stratosphere of world politics to sustain so daring an adventure. The answer to that question could not be immediately forthcoming, and the good fortune which saved the world at that stage lay in the fact that there were a half dozen great and enlightened spirits like Lord Robert Cecil, Smuts, Briand, and Stresemann, who shook off the shackles of the past while it was still too soon fully to comprehend the possibilities of the present or the menace of the future. Under their leadership in the great nations, powerfully supported by Branting, Nansen, Benes, and others who trooped the small nations back of the ideal, the League of Nations became a going concern, the World Court was firmly established, the Treaties of

Locarno were made, and it became possible to enunciate the principle of the Briand-Kellogg Pact which, on paper at least, reverses the fundamental principle of international relations as it had been expounded and defended from the beginning of recorded history. Such informed criticism as there is of these new institutions deals largely with matters of detail. There is nowhere in the world any responsible suggestion that they are not fundamentally right, and the people of the United States, above all others in the world, should abide their development and improvement by evolutionary processes with the greatest patience and confidence.

In our own history, it took us ten years, under the Articles of Confederation, to realize the need of a more perfect union, and in the nearly one hundred and fifty years since our constitution was adopted, we have seen it grow and expand beyond the dreams or plans of its founders, acquiring new meanings as new conditions arose, and demonstrating always fresh vitality and adequacy. People who have seen great oaks grown from acorns have no right to doubt what time and good will and patience will bring out of these great beginnings. If I have attributed this progress in too great degree to the fortunate accident of the existence of these great personalities, I am not unaware of the presence of irresistible forces at work to aid them. The logic of events is stronger than the wills of men, and conditions, dimly perceived before the World War, have moved with accelerated speed and accumulated momentum in the same direction. The proposal of these great institutions, dedicated to the preservation of the peace of the world, would have been regarded as ''mere idealism,'' proceeding from an academic assumption of the perfectibility of the race, but for the fact that they have actually been set up, and have been in successful operation for now ten years. And these facts demonstrate that, among nations as among individuals, ideals have a better chance when we are poor than when we are rich. When the tide of national expansion and colonial acquisition was on, and the possibility of outstripping one's rivals in the armament race still held out the illusory hope of security if not supremacy, nations were not likely to pass self-denying ordinances or to join in arrangements which denied, by anticipation, the victory and the spoils thereof to the strong. But the first great revelation of the World War was that the strongest nation, under modern conditions, dies, like a bee, when it uses its sting. The second great revelation of the World War was undoubtedly the universality of the disaster. The song of the victor, as he contemplated his victim sitting in the ashes of desolation, died in his throat when he remembered the cost of his victory. This was a revelation not to princes and potentates, or to statesmen and generals, but to peoples. There were too many widow's weeds mingled with the torchbearers in the victory parade, too many *mutilés* seeking limited readmission to factories and workshops, particularly there was too much dislocation in the processes of international industry and finance to permit any nation to feel itself safe from an overwhelming share in the common disaster. Out of realizations of this general kind came that loss of faith which, for a time, was the most menacing consequence of the whole experience. Political systems which had been impotent to prevent the catastrophe came under a distrust so deep that they were, with practically no exception, replaced with substitutes of popular origin and theoretically resting on popular sanction.

That these new political institutions have taken varying forms is part of our present problem. The discussions here presented of capitalism, fascism, and communism, the latter two as represented by Italy and Russia respectively, in an effort to study out the form of social organization best adapted to meet the demands of modern industrial conditions, suggest a question thought debatable, as to whether the institutions of the past are either suited to, or could be made to suit, present and immediately future conditions. In the consideration of such a question, it seems to me important to have in mind the fact that modern industrialism is very modern, while the political institutions of most of the settled countries of the world are in part an inheritance evolved from centuries of experience and adapted to national temperament; hence, while it is relatively easy to set up a new factory, it is incredibly difficult to set up a new form of government. The lines which industrial and economic development shall take are determined and tested by concrete and practical experiences, while the political developments of the people, to be suitable at all, must rest upon an historical foundation and be adjusted to emotional responses which have their origin in racial characteristics and are conditioned by linguistic, religious, and philosophical associations. New forms, established by revolutions, are easily forgotten in times of stress, and the tendency of peoples is to revert to traditional forms when a new and academic institution experiences temporary difficulties. Even compact and contiguous bodies of people, living long under one general government, speaking the same language and having identical external interests, preserve with amazing stubbornness racial and temperamental differences. England and Scotland were united under the same crown in the days of James the First, and Wales became a part of the United Kingdom centuries ago; they have a common parliament, a common army and navy and diplomatic service, to a substantial extent a common literature and a common culture, and yet they are still, respectively, England, Scotland, and Wales. As it is true that the political and industrial institutions of a people interact, consideration must be given to both of them if any attempt is to be made either to gauge or measurably to control the future.

On the political side, the most important change in world conditions has been the disappearance of autocratic and dynastic systems of government and the subjection of the world to democratic influences, even where the forms adopted seem undemocratic. One immediate effect of this is the necessary replacement of the old diplomatic procedures by processes of open discussion. Probably no one of the Fourteen Points enunciated by President Wilson caused more condescending smiles by its apparent *naïveté* than that which demanded open covenants, openly arrived at, but certainly no statement ever made by him was more prescient or sagacious, for, if the world is to be governed by its peoples, which the growth of the democratic theory implies, that must ultimately and soon come to be the method of international arrangements. The whole mechanism by

which understandings, ententes, and alliances used
to be made will have to be, and is being, revised, and
things which will not bear the light of day and free
discussion will have to be abandoned. Secret treaties
and undisclosed obligations cannot be made by
statesmen whose only power is delegated by people
who consent to nothing as to which they are not
fully informed. Even before the World War this result of the democratic theory was making itself
felt—the British statesmen who undertook to consider combinations with France to meet contingen-
cies which might arise did not venture to go beyond
"conversations," and when in the opinion of these
statesmen vital interests of Great Britain were affected by the evolution of the war, the people of the
British Empire could not be summoned to take sides
in deference to any understanding previously arrived at. The difference between the German Em-
peror mobilizing to support Austria as his ally, and
Sir Edward Grey explaining to the British Parliament the situation which had developed, with patient fulness of detail and deep embarrassment lest
the government had committed Parliament or the
people against their freedom of choice, is an excellent illustration of the difference between the two
theories and procedures. Perhaps an even better
illustration is afforded by the action of American
public opinion upon certain fantastic stories circulated here after the outbreak of the war to the effect
that there were understandings between our Government and Great Britain or our Government and
France. The plain man in the street shrugged his
shoulders and pointed to that provision in the Constitution which vests the treaty-making power in the

President, by and with the advice and consent of the Senate, and went his way with no sense of possible obligation growing out of any usurpation of power by the Washington Government. It is a recognition of this fact which led General Smuts to say that the Versailles Treaty, made by statesmen, would be completed and amended by peoples. This is the fact which is at the very basis of the idea of the League of Nations, where treaties are matters of public record and free discussion is the mechanism of adjustment. This fact underlies all agencies which are nowadays suggested for the adjustment of international disputes: arbitration, conference, conciliation, and adjudication. All imply candid expositions of facts and anticipate the acceptance of awards, compromises, and judgments through the pressure of an informed public opinion.

I have for a long time believed that the United States ought to declare as a fundamental doctrine of its national policy that it will not trade with any nation at war which has been declared, by a competent tribunal, to be the aggressor. The so-called Burton and Capper resolutions, so far as they go, seem to me to declare the moral sense of the people of the United States, and as most of the important nations of the world are already bound by treaties which accept either the League, or arbitrators to be agreed upon, as competent authorities to pass upon such a disputed question, I have had no difficulty in foreseeing such a policy in effective operation. No such formal declaration of our national policy has been made by the Government, but I think it has been made by the people of the United States, and it is my belief that if a war were to break out anywhere in the world between nations which have agreed to submit their controversies to arbitration, and have agreed upon an agency to ascertain the facts and declare, as between them, which is the aggressor, public opinion in the United States would force our Government to acquiesce in such a decision and to withhold the support of our resources, public and private, from the aggressor. In this instance I am confident that public opinion has anticipated and preceded governmental action and that whether any such policy is declared or not, no nation, which aggressively breaks the peace of the world, will find it possible to rely upon American industry or American finance for support, or upon the American Government for any benevolence in its neutrality.

The part which "peoples" are to play, and are playing, in the readjustment of the world is further illustrated by the extent to which there have grown up in all countries voluntary agencies to study international relations and, by informing public opinion, mobilize it in support of the institutions established by the statesmen, as the formal expression of the new method. The popular literature on the subject of international relations, in every country in the world, has become literally vast in volume. The number of associations, leagues, institutes, forums, surveys, and study groups established abroad for this purpose is not only evidence of the assertion by the public of their interest in what was before regarded as the mystery of statecraft, but it is an assurance to the statesmen of these several countries that the democracies back of them are being kept informed and are watchfully sympathetic with every move which is made in the new spirit. The situation in the

United States presents an especially interesting and impressive picture. Our Government has preached and practiced isolation. Those in places of official responsibility have evidently believed that public opinion in the United States turned resolutely in 1918 from any further interest in our political relations with the rest of the world, and they have accordingly accompanied every official manifestation of interest with meticulous and painstaking explanations as to the limitations of the proposed action and its consistency with the rigid maintenance of isolation as a national policy. Meanwhile, the people of the United States have gone far ahead of their government. Great and enlightened American citizens have, as individuals, participated in and aided practically all of the constructive work undertaken by the League of Nations. Official representatives of the United States have, of course, "unofficially," been likewise coöperative and helpful. The services rendered by such men as Elihu Root, Charles G. Dawes, Owen D. Young, and the experts whom they grouped about them, and expositors of the new mechanisms which have been set up by the new spirit in international affairs like James T. Shotwell and others, have been a peculiarly American contribution, obviously detached and disinterested, and as obviously weighty because of the great experience and learning and the devotion of spirit with which these services have been rendered. Meanwhile, in the United States, there have grown up scores of foundations, unions, associations, leagues, and societies, most of them of national scope which seek to inform and concentrate the opinion of great bodies of our people upon problems presented by the new world

order. Many of these societies, of course, are highly
specialized in their objective, many of them are
limited in their field to members of particular religious faiths, or academic, social, or political groups,
but, taken together, they manifest a new public interest in international affairs, and the very names
of many of these groups imply a recognition of community of interest among the peoples of the world
in large areas of action and thought which, prior to
the World War, would have been regarded as of
local or national concern. A striking instance of the
effect of all this was seen when President Hoover
suddenly, and without preliminary preparation of
the public mind, announced his plan for a morato-
rium upon German reparation payments and payments among the former allies upon the so-called
War Debts. Continuously, for several years prior to
this announcement, official Washington had set its
face against any reconsideration or modification of
the so-called debt settlement and it resolutely asserted that German reparation payments had no relation to payments under the American debt settlement, and would not be considered as being in any
way related to them. International groups proposing
to open this subject for discussion were discouraged
from expecting any willingness on the part of the
Government of the United States to interest itself in
the reparations question or to recognize anything
but complete finality in the settlement it had made
of its War debts. There could be no doubt that
Washington listened with an anxious ear when the
situation in Germany became such that immediate
and drastic action, which no country but the United
States was in a position to take, became necessary

to save the whole European industrial and financial situation. And if there was joy there must also have been surprise when it was discovered that the people of the United States had long since reached a conclusion upon a subject which Washington, until then, had declined to consider, and that the action of the President, completely at variance with all the doctrines and fixed resolutions proclaimed from Washington, was not only heartily welcomed and approved, but by unanimous consent was declared to be the most conspicuous act of high statesmanship in his career. The approval which greeted the action of the President was not limited to groups whose opinion might be regarded as specially well informed—our so-called political intelligentsia—or to groups whose financial interests might give them special concern over the prospect of serious disturbance in the international financial structure. Those who noted the reception accorded the President's proposal by plain men had the experience of hearing artisans and small business men spontaneously evidencing their understanding and approval.

Whether or not the action taken by the President might not have been taken much earlier may well be questioned, and there are those who find it difficult to believe that a situation which, like this, threatens to affect the whole financial and political situation in the world, should be allowed to develop to the point where instant, unprepared, and unexpected action is necessary to prevent revolution or repudiation in a matter of hours. Questions like these have been and should be put aside for the moment. This is the time to coöperate and not to criticize. Public opinion in the United States has rarely shown itself steadier, more competent, or more restrained than in this critical moment when, if the world is to be saved, action was necessary and criticism could only result in weakening the helpful forces at last stirred to action. This is all very reassuring, for it shows that our democracy is educating itself, and is prepared to sustain and vitalize the agencies which the statesmen have set up for ordering world affairs. It indicates that the "peoples" to whom General Smuts looked for the amendment of the treaty can be relied upon to work out that happy result. It ought to be reassuring, too, to statesmen who have to deal officially with the contentious questions growing out of the treaty arrangements. Apparently they can, with confidence, bring these questions into the open for public discussion, propose open methods for their reconsideration, and rely upon public opinion to sustain the wise revisions when expert research has supplied the information necessary for the formation of sound popular judgments. Questions like the Anschluss, the Hungarian frontiers, and the Polish Corridor will be sooner and better settled by that method than by indirect approaches through customs unions, and private suggestions between the interested nations. The people seem to remember, even if the statesmen may have forgotten, that the treaties were made not only to settle past controversies, but to arrange future opportunities, and it is, after all, less important to remember ancient grudges and cherish ancient fears than it is to create a brave and liberal atmosphere in which nations can live their future.

But we must not forget as we march into this new era of democratic influences and democratic power that there are grave dangers and responsibilities attending it. Appenzell is, of course, the only pure democracy, and it can exist and function only because it is so small. With every increase in numbers, with every increase of the area occupied, with every increased diversity of occupation and interest in a democracy, the problem of informing public opinion and restraining impetuous and ill-advised action and giving expression to deliberate judgments increases. In 1884, James Russell Lowell made his address on democracy in Birmingham. Stout champion as he was of democracy as a theory of political organization, he nevertheless pointed out that the success of our own democratic experiment was most open to doubt in our great cities where congested masses of men, busy to the point of exhaustion about their own concerns and having little time for meditation, were especially subject to heady and emotional action—to have, as he phrased it, their emotions "trooped" by slogans and to be led into passionate movements before the facts were all bared or discussed or perhaps even known. Lowell, in a footnote to his address, commented on the fact that we had yet to learn the effect of the electric telegraph in conveying information simultaneously to great bodies of people. Since 1884 this difficulty has increased. Great central news organizations have been established which supply hourly to the world such views of the facts as their agents can procure in hurried competitive searches for important happenings. To the electric telegraph and cable we have added the wireless, and an impatient and impulsive word, delivered in the heat of an extemporaneous speech by an important stateman, blazes provoca-

tively within an hour in headlines in every part of
the world or penetrates our private homes over the
radio, undigested and unmodified by the conciliatory phrases which may have followed five minutes
later in the same speech. That the formation of
sound public opinion is, under these circumstances,
beset by peculiar dangers is clear. There can be no
guardianship for a whole people. There is no tol-
erable censorship in such matters. Public opinion
will form itself on whatever facts it has; sound public opinion cannot be based on less than all the facts.
When public opinion thus becomes the dominant
force in the affairs of men, the responsibility on the
part of the people for seeing that that opinion shall
be sound is immeasurably important. The obvious
answer to this danger is that democracy, realizing
its power, must learn to use it responsibly. In *Little Dorrit*, Dickens illustrates the point by telling
us of Tattycoram, a little serving maid with an impulsive temper and an explosive tongue. Her wise
employer, whenever he saw her about to break out,
always said to her quietly "count five and twenty,
Tattycoram," with the result that when five and
twenty had been deliberately counted, the passion
had evaporated. We should acquire the international
habit of "counting five and twenty." The statesmen
have set up the machinery and the people are taking
over its operation, or, at least, its successful operation depends upon an approving consent of the
people. Education in the facts of our modern international life and culture in a broad and tolerant and
unselfish spirit is necessary to make life under modern conditions possible, and comprises the discipline
to which we, as citizens, must subject ourselves. This

may sound like a long road, but it is the only safe
road. Each international incident as it arises becomes an educational opportunity when it is approached in this spirit. Conferences for the limitation of naval armament, for instance, have none of
them really gone to the root of the matter of the
folly and danger of competitive building, but they
have served an immense educational purpose. The
great disarmament conference to be held next year
will meet in a sounder atmosphere, and the delegates who attend it will be braver, because of the
difficulties and failures which have gone before. The
strong likelihood is that by the time the disarmament conference comes, every delegate there will
have learned from the people of his country that
the public have little patience with technical difficulties and excuses, thinly disguising nationalistic pre-
tensions. The public opinion of the world will wel-
come and support those bold spirits who, when that
conference meets, proclaim as its guiding principle
that the way to disarm is to disarm.

I have noted that the program of this Institute
proposes for discussion both political and economic
questions. On the economic side, the problem presented is whether under modern conditions world
economics can be permitted to develop without a
plan. In large part this thought derives from the so-
called Five Year Plan which Russia has promulgated and widely advertised. Varying opinions are
still possible about the success of the October Revolution in Russia. That it has managed to survive
may be due to a combination of any number of a
dozen causes which have little to do with its soundness as an economic or political philosophy. That it

has not yet produced an economic millennium is no
more an indictment of it than a like failure of capitalism, which still has its storms and stresses, its
tale of waste and human derelicts. At the present
moment it is difficult to tell what the Russian situation is or what it is becoming. The recent announcement from Moscow that it is necessary to establish
a difference between the reward for skilled work,
well done, and unskilled work, slovenly done, has a
familiar sound to those who have clung to some
form of capitalistic organization in the belief that
under all conditions individual initiative must be
preserved, and virtue permitted to win its own
award. But Russia has asked the rest of the world
several disconcerting, if not destructive questions,
which it may be that she herself has not yet satisfactorily answered, but which challenge us to try
to answer them about our own situation. At the out-
set it is important to point out that any analogy between the Russian Five Year Plan and a possible
plan for the world economic progress is misleading.
Russia is planning to catch up. The rest of the nations of the world are considering the possibility of
planning to go forward. Russia, as an economically
and industrially backward nation, is planning to attain the sort of productive competence already attained by others, but for an already great industrial
nation to plan its future development is a very different thing, and whether there can be wisdom
enough to plan an economic future for the United
States or for the world seems very doubtful indeed.
History gives us some examples in the past of what
Russia is doing today. They are unlabeled and un-
advertised but they are real parallels. After the in-

dustrial age had established itself in Great Britain and much of the cost and experience of developing machine production had been borne, Germany determined to become an industrial nation and did it by importing machinery, practices, and methods from England, thus making the starting point of her own technical development the proved results of British experiments and experience. An even more striking illustration is afforded by the case of Japan, an entirely alien nation with none of the industrial traditions with which even Germany started. By taking over the best that had been developed in England, Germany, and the United States, the Japanese built a technology and became an industrial nation in an incredibly short space of time. In neither of these instances was there a Five Year Plan or an announced or advertised program, but the thing was essentially the same as that which Russia is now doing with its installation of hydro-electric power, its introduction of Ford plants, and its adoption of the most up-to-date agricultural and industrial machinery and practices. All three of the incidents are imitative and in each case the start is made under the most favorable auspices, for the countries which have developed the new techniques are left with all of the costs and burdens of development as clogs upon their industry, while the new entrant into the industrial field escapes the griefs and burdens of experimentation and development and makes its starting point the best that its competitors have been able to do, unencumbered by the history of their efforts. The exercise by Russia of a tyrannous political control as a means of subjecting the Russian people to the sacrifices necessary to achieve quickly the indus-

trial competence of the western world is obviously
only a temporary and transitory phenomenon. The
inefficiency of slave labor is an axiom, and whether
the servitude be imposed by a whip or a dogma, will
not change the great truth that no form of social
organization can endure, or is indeed worth seeking,
which does not leave room for the individual man.
The problem of world economic planning is, however, as I have said, an entirely different thing. Economic progress in the past has been an evolution—
the cut and try method has been its characteristic.
In industry and economics, as in the world of more
abstract ideas, the daring have pushed up against
the wall of the unachieved, finding either a soft spot
which it was possible to break through to greater
progress, or a hard and unyielding place from which
it was necessary to recoil for efforts in other directions. It has been found impossible, so far, to make
any coherent and promising plan for the organization of some of our own domestic industries of a
fundamental kind. For instance, neither England
nor the United States has been able to organize the
coal industry, or to make any plan for organizing it,
which gives the slightest promise of placing this
most fundamental industrial occupation upon a
sound economic basis either as to production or consumption, or to introduce into it either stability for
its owners or dignified and adequate lives for its
workers. Industrial progress is made by the development of new things, but new things upset the equi-
librium of any plan. Who could have planned the industrial effects of the development of the railroads,
or the economic changes which we have seen attend
the development of the internal combustion engine?

Obviously, unless we are prepared to put world economics in a strait-jacket, and, like the encyclopedists, write its final history on the theory that further progress is impossible, no such plan could be made for nations which are forging ahead as is entirely rational for nations which are still catching up.

This, however, does not mean that the world must sit still and take what comes from an unstudied and unregulated play of economic and industrial forces. The experience of the race, which is a sounder reliance than the wisdom of any generation, has shown us that progress is a function of freedom. While we may not definitely plan the direction or speed of progress, we can coöperate in efforts to establish those conditions of freedom under which progress is possible. Of these conditions I shall, for a moment, ask your attention to but two. The first and most essential is, of course, the effective establishment of peace in international relations. All progress is an illusion if there impends over it the possibility of the disaster of world war. Even so vast and intricate and beautiful a thing as civilization can commit suicide like an individual. Modern war is a loaded pistol, aimed at the heart of civilization itself with its hair-trigger held by an unsteady hand. The approaching disarmament conference will probably show us whether the size and destructive power of that pistol is to be increased or decreased, or the hand rendered more unsteady. Curiously enough, the controlling voices at that conference will be the voices of the great nations which have armed on the theory of offensive preponderance as a defensive measure, but the question to be decided by the conference is not whether this or that nation, by obstinate insistence upon momentary military strength, can achieve, at the expense of traditional enemies, some territorial or economic advantage, but rather whether the pride and obstinacy of some particular nations will force the world to live in a powder magazine until the final explosion sweeps away the strong and the weak alike. The hope of the disarmament conference lies not in the statesmen of the world but in the peoples of the world, and the strength of the peoples of the world at that conference depends not upon the knowledge or good will of a few elect and thoughtful spirits, but in the extent to which popular knowledge is thorough and deep and so fortifies the representatives of the people with the support of an informed and resolute public opinion.

Upon the purely economic side I find the other suggestion which I desire to bring to your attention. One of the astonishing consequences of the reorganization of Europe by the Treaty of Versailles has been the growth of barrier tariffs. The nations of pre-war Europe were organized in a measure at least on the theory of an identity of economic interest modified by dynastic aspirations. At Versailles, the principle of nationalities was substituted, with the consequence that the freshly emancipated peoples were launched as nations with the double duty of establishing new political institutions and new economic policies. That an extreme nationalistic turn should have been given to both of these tasks is not strange but the results are obviously unfortunate. The old ties and dependencies were gone. To have attempted to reëstablish them and keep them

separate from political implications would have
been too great a task, even had the wisdom of the
moment been enough to permit its importance to be
seen. I shall not go into any statistical illustration of
just what has been done. It is fair to say that barrier
tariffs have been erected on every new frontier and
many of them are provocative, some of them frankly
hostile, and all of them an encumbrance upon that
field of freedom in which progress and peace can
best function. The spirit in which many of these
tariffs have been enacted has been the war spirit
and while it is too much to hope that there can be
any immediate economic counterpart to the Briand-
Kellogg Pact, by which the nations will agree not
to use the tariff as an instrument of national policy,
it is yet clear that we cannot go on declaring economic war upon each other, ruthlessly wrecking
each other's industries, and disorganizing each
other's economic systems, without ultimately producing the kind of friction out of which many of the
wars of the past have been generated. This is ad-
mittedly a difficult and refractory subject, and any
approach to it must take cognizance of the fact that
the existing social and economic organization of
each nation is a status, to some extent artificially
attained through years of reliance upon national
economic policies. To ask a sudden reversal of these
policies, or any drastic change in them, would entail
more domestic disorganization than nations are willing to confront. Many nations, including the United
States, may find, as a result of the present economic
depression, that stimulation of their own foreign
trade would be furthered by reducing their tariffs,
but from an international point of view we cannot

afford to wait upon a process so sporadic and gradual as this is for it depends upon, practically, the reëducation in every country of the whole body of public opinion which has been committed to the use of tariffs as a legitimate expression of nationalism in economic competition. Plainly, such reëducations in each country, from its own domestic point of view, ought to be encouraged and there seems little doubt that they will be undertaken. But the world as a whole needs a plan of gradual contemporaneous emancipation from the past, a method which will tend to preserve, relatively, the economic conditions and reliances of the several nations, but which will bring about, over a long period of years, an approach to freedom if not equality of economic opportunity. In my judgment this method cannot be sought by conferences dealing with items in tariff schedules. The confusion incident to a general tariff revision in any country is sufficiently discouraging, but simultaneous general tariff revision in all countries, even if they were attempted in conformity with some general principles arrived at by international conference, is unthinkable. Each country would have its own legislation await the outcome of legislative action in every other country where its export interests were substantial. It would be difficult to arrive, by any general consensus, upon the fundamental principles of tariff making. The separate schedules are often of interest to a relatively small number of countries but of no general interest, and the confusion of attempting to work out these special interests by contemporaneous legislative provisions makes the whole problem unapproachable by that method. Another difficulty would arise from the fact that such a plan contemplates a day when all this harmonized legislation would come into effect; that is, a day at which and from which practically the entire economic structure of the world would start on a new basis. Perhaps it is enough to say that things are not done that way and cannot be. But it is still possible to suggest a plan of gradual approach. We once had a tariff in the United States which provided for a gradual reduction to a maximum of twenty per cent by annual horizontal reductions in all schedules containing, as originally enacted, a duty in excess of that amount. This seems to me to hold out a very practical suggestion. An international conference could assume that the present status of the tariff legislation of each country represents its present policy relative to all other nations with which it sustains trade relations. Such a conference could recommend, for general adoption, legislation in all countries, making horizontal reductions in all schedules, to go into effect simultaneously, at definite rates over periods of years, calculated to permit the effect of the reduction to be absorbed by domestic readjustments. This would preserve the relative situation of all countries. It would meet the national prejudice against unilateral economic disarmament. It could be done much more rapidly than by any other process because no country would be put in any changed relative relation to other countries, and all countries would know in advance the extent and rate of change and so be able to busy themselves to meet the changes as they went into effect. The final advantage of this plan seems to me to lie in the fact that it does not subject the tariff policy of any nation to

international control which would run counter to
the insuperable obstacles of that national feeling
which has, in every country, always insisted that
tariff making is a domestic question. I do not speak
as an economist and, in the life of a busy practicing
lawyer, I obviously have not the time to devote to
the study and the acquiring of expert training necessary to entitle one to speak with authority about
this question.

Political institutions, it seems to me, cannot be
wisely subjected to sudden and revolutionary
change. We cannot tear ourselves loose from our
history and adopt unfamiliar and exotic political arrangements merely because they have been found
congenial to other peoples and better adapted to
their situations and needs. We can, however, modify
our political arrangements to facilitate our economic
development and that process has gone on continuously in our own country and in every other country
with a modern civilization. In like manner we can
modify our economic systems and bring them more
into harmony with the theories upon which in this
new age our political institutions are based. Our
own capitalistic system obviously needs modification. The alternations to which we are at present
subjected, between periods of surfeit and periods
of widespread unemployment and want, subject the
life of people who do the world's work to hardship
and hazard inconsistent with the demands of a
stable social order and too cruel in its effects to be
patiently accepted. On the other hand, to fly from
what we have to a system which has so far resulted
in a mere hope of an ultimate economic competence,
by a drastic subjection of the people to a system of

compulsory and uncompensated servitude, invites social instability from another cause. There is room in the world for many political systems, there is room in the world for many economic theories. Historical, geographical, and racial differences among men are too great to permit it to be supposed that any one set of political institutions or one set of economic theories could be equally serviceable among them all.

This does not mean a supine acceptance of events as they may happen nor does it mean a narrow and restricted view of either the functions or possibilities of government under modern conditions. In a simpler age, there grew up the doctrine of *laissez faire* as an expression of a view that if the government would but keep its hands off, individual initiative and vigor would achieve the best results. And it is still possible to believe in less government rather than more government as the answer for many of our ills. But we must not blind ourselves to the fact that the increasing intricacy of human relations necessitates increasing accommodations and concessions and that this is just as true of nations in the international network as it is of individuals in the domestic social fabric. There are large areas of new relations, or old relations expanded into new importance and meaning, as to which conscious regulation is the effective answer. As to international things, the world has certainly entered the coöperative age and the progress and future welfare of the world are to be sought in matters of high common concern by consultation, agreement, and coöperative efforts. There is, however, a vast difference between coöperation and coalescence. In the domestic society there must be room for the individual man, and in international society there must be room for the individual nation. Some part of our national feeling may be *amour propre,* but when all allowances are made there remains such a thing as national culture, a kind of culture that cannot as yet be attained without the stimulation of national feeling, and which has great mental and spiritual and physical gifts to contribute to the world's progress. A rough statement of the ideal at which we ought to aim is, therefore, coöperating individuals in a series of domestic societies which themselves remain individual but coöperate about their common concerns.

That I have selected only two illustrations of the world's present need of coöperative activity does not mean that there are not countless others of greater or less concern. The two I have used, however, are obviously dominant in the respective fields of politics and economics, and the spirit in which I have sought to approach them seems to me a spirit in which our common lesser problems may be hopefully approached. Our planning should seek to establish the reign of justice in the interrelations of independent peoples and to free their economic efforts from restraints and obstacles imposed in the spirit of conquest which, in the modern world, would naturally be in the economic field.

I have not attempted to catalogue all the social ills and problems which need consideration but I have attempted to produce the reflections of a man in the street and to summarize for the information of experts the state of education and determination to which public opinion seems to me to have arrived.

The gravity of the problems which we face needs no emphasis. The tragedy of failure in their solution is sufficiently illustrated by the recent economic and political history of Europe and America. That a new spirit has come in matters of international concern, and in the new technique which has been evolved for the consideration of international problems, whether economic or political, is the point I try to make, and in it I find immense stimulation and encouragement. The world has been rocked in a great storm and even yet the winds and the floods have not abated. Modern civilization is worth preserving, hence the essential soundness of the craft in which we are embarked has been demonstrated. Some strong hands have been discovered to be at the wheel, and, in the darkness, some lights are already appearing, which seems to indicate that at the end of a great striving we may hope for safe port.

APPENDIX

DISCUSSION OF THE ECONOMIC SYSTEMS OF FASCISM, COMMUNISM, AND CAPITALISM

First Conference

CHAIRMAN BLAKESLEE: We have now had six very interesting and valuable addresses presenting the economic systems of Fascism, Sovietism and Capitalism, and we shall proceed to two general discussions on these subjects. We trust that the question-and-answer form of discussion will bring out the strong and weak points of each system; and perhaps we shall find that they hold some lessons for our country.

The first question is from Dr. Villari to Dr. Counts:

"If a differentiation is made between good and bad workers, between the skilled and the less skilled, will not the differences of class and the economic position be restored?"

DR. GEORGE S. COUNTS: Undoubtedly such distinctions will be reflected, I think, in differences in social position between the economic and social order, but until they take the form of control of property, I do not believe they will amount to very much. Stalin's recent speech recognizes these distinctions, although they have existed for a good many years, and that fact should be kept in mind. At the present time one cannot own the tools of production—natural resources or land—and until the Communists make concessions on those points, I do not think there is very much danger of the development of classes in the sense in which we use the term.

However, there is one point, I think, in the Soviet system in which there may be some danger in this direction. That is not the distinction based upon property or upon income, but the distinction based upon membership in the party. It is the distinction between the party member and the non-party member that is important in Russia today, and not differences in compensation.

CHAIRMAN BLAKESLEE: Here is a question addressed to Colonel Rorty: "Does Fascism have an advantage over capitalism in the quickness and the ease with which it can bring about needed changes in the price level of wages and commodities?"

COLONEL RORTY: It seems to me the answer to that very clearly is "yes." The only qualification that counts is whether or not the restraints of Fascism represent too high a price to pay for this economic flexibility.

CHAIRMAN BLAKESLEE: I have another question addressed to Colonel Rorty: "Does state socialism eliminate a large amount of waste inevitable under capitalism?"

COLONEL RORTY: I think there again the answer is "yes." I am assuming that the question relates to individual competitive capitalism. State socialism will undoubtedly eliminate much waste inevitable under capitalism. However, this answer means nothing. First of all, much waste is desirable, rather than undesirable. It is a very moderate price we pay for growth and evolution. Most of our constant increases in productivity are the result of doing the right thing by wastefully doing the wrong things. At the time of the millennium we will develop a race of supermen who can do things in the best way on their first attempt. Until that time we have the choice only between the progress and wastes of individual initiative, and the regularity of mediocre methods.

CHAIRMAN BLAKESLEE: Dr. Villari, in his lecture, said: "The economic system of Fascism is closely bound up with the political aspects of the movement." I think it is due to that statement that Colonel Rorty asks him, "What system is contemplated for succession to Mussolini?"

DR. LUIGI VILLARI: A foreign friend of mine, also a personal friend of Signor Mussolini, has replied to that question that there would be a magnificent funeral, beautiful flowers, speeches of moving eloquence—and in a fortnight's time things would go on as before.

But there is also a legal or constitutional answer. By the law of the Fascist Grand Council the Grand Council drafts a list of names which it keeps up to date, of persons regarded as suitable successors in case of death or retirement of the present Prime Minister. This list would be submitted to the King, and he would send for the man whom he regarded as most acceptable. This clause was drafted by Mussolini himself.

Naturally the disappearance of a man of genius would be a loss to the country. But there are in Italy today enough men of ability to make it possible to find a successor.

MR. GEORGE C. PERKINS, NEWARK, NEW YORK: "Does Fascism seek to limit the accumulation of private property, and if so, to what extent?"

DR. VILLARI: No, there is no limitation to the accumulation of private property, provided that it is brought about honestly. The accumulation of private property brought about in other ways is liable to punishment by law in Italy as in other civilized countries.

CHAIRMAN BLAKESLEE: Another question to Dr. Villari, from Colonel Rorty: "Is there a middle ground between dictatorship and popular government?"

DR. VILLARI: The question might have been answered in the negative before the war, but today there are so many variations and shades of variations in the forms of governments that it is impossible to divide them into cut and dried categories. The same government, moreover, may be a dictatorship in one sense, a popular government in a second, and another type of government in a third. The present government in Italy may be described as a popular dictatorship because the powers have been conferred upon Mussolini by popular will.

RABBI SOLOMON FOSTER, NEW JERSEY NORMAL SCHOOL FOR JEWISH TEACHERS: In their lectures both Dr. Counts and Dr. Villari referred to the Communist Party and the Fascist Party without going into details. I should like to ask each of these gentlemen what constitutes membership in the Communist Party and in the Fascist Party, what privileges membership entails, and what authority do these parties wield over their respective systems?

DR. VILLARI: In a few words, membership in the Fascist Party places a man in a position of moral privilege and he is given, other things being equal, certain advantages. Nonmembership however does not exclude persons from different branches of the civil service. No member of the military services may be a Fascist, because it is traditional that the Italian fighting services have always been regarded as definitely outside of party; a man in the fighting services must be a non-party man, therefore he cannot be a Fascist.

In the other branches of the service there are a great many non-Fascists. The Fascists, as a rule, are given the preference over members of parties not Fascists, but the practice, I believe, is not peculiar to Italy. I believe there are other countries where, if you are a member of a certain party, you enjoy certain advantages.

DR. COUNTS: To speak briefly: The Communist Party does rule Soviet Russia. There is no question about that; no one in Russia, whether a member of the party or outside of it, denies it. The party today consists of about two million members. It is supported by two groups of younger persons, a Young Communist Party of about 3,000,000 members, enrolling young people between the ages of thirteen and twenty-three, and another party called the Pioneers, which enrolls youngsters from ten to thirteen, with a present enrollment of about four millions.

Membership in the party is dependent upon a number of considerations. You must apply, and you are put on probation. How long the probation will be depends upon your occupation. The party, of course, favors membership from the proletariat and makes an effort to remain strongly proletarian. It endeavors to have at least 50 per cent of its membership made up of persons coming directly from the bench. It also endeavors to get membership from among the poor and middle-class peasants.

If you ask a Communist what his privileges are, he will tell you "none; only responsibilities." If you are a member of the party you are expected to devote from ten to thirty hours a week to labor without compensation. Your compensation, if you are gifted, will probably be limited to less than you would get if you were not a member of the party. The most you can get as a member of the party is 300 rubles a month; engineers not members of the party may get 1,500 or 2,000 rubles a month. On the other hand, there is a certain prestige that goes with membership, accompanied undoubtedly by certain power.

CHAIRMAN BLAKESLEE: A question to Professor Counts from Dr. Villari: "Will Russian industry, artificially created, in an essentially agricultural atmosphere and in primitive conditions amidst a population unaccustomed to industrial life, punctuality and precision, be able to compete with the better organized industry of the west, at all events for several generations?"

DR. COUNTS: I think there is real point to the question and I agree in general with its implications. However, as to how long this is going to take, nobody knows. It is wholly a matter of guesswork. I don't know that there has been a case in history where such a concerted effort has been made to lift a population out of a simple, primitive, agrarian order into an industrial order, and I know of no case where all the instruments of education, all the forces that mold the lives of a population, are being brought to bear upon a population to accomplish this end.

I would say that it is going to take some time to produce in Russia the more complicated and finer types of industrial products. At the present time Russia is competing with the western nations in Manchuria, Mongolia, and some of the border states, in the production of cheap manufactured goods, but in the production of the higher quality of goods I think there is little danger of competition for a considerable time. I would not place it beyond a generation; perhaps it will be even less.

The CHAIRMAN then called upon Mr. Albert M. Creighton, Director of the National Shawmut Bank, of Boston, to give his observations from a recent trip to Russia.

MR. CREIGHTON: I was in Russia during April and May of this year, and was interested to learn what progress had been made in the plants since my previous visits in 1926 particularly, and in 1929. We went into the factories and into the plants, and we felt that we went unhampered. We talked with the peasants in the fields, and with the farmers, and later with the workers in the factories.

The first factory that we went through was a shoe factory in Moscow—a business I had been interested in for some years. I found that they were working far better than they had been working in 1926. They were making 20,000 pairs of shoes a day—the same shoes over and over and over throughout the year, without change of style and in only two widths. The workers did not even raise their heads as we walked through the plants. You would hardly find such concentration as that in America. They were working two shifts a day, seven hours for each shift, producing shoes of about the quality of those produced in America after the Civil War. No one would care to wear them here, but they are the kind to produce there where only 70,000,-000 pairs of shoes are made per year for 160,000,000 people.

Spread over the walls in every direction were great banners urging the workers to compete with other factories, and to beat factories located elsewhere.

In that factory I felt that the efficiency was much greater than in 1926, although in some of the plants I visited, particularly those making agricultural machinery, I found the efficiency very low.

From Moscow we went to Kiev, where we visited what is known as the "Hollywood of the Ukraine." The moving picture plant there was built wholly by the Germans, and runs at a fair efficiency. The films produced are about 75 per cent propaganda. The stars receive from three to four hundred rubles, or $150 to $200 a month, while the directors receive four to five hundred rubles a month.

Everywhere throughout the nation the piece-work basis prevails and there are in the different plants anywhere from ten to fifteen different grades of labor. The more skilled receive perhaps three or four hundred rubles a month, and those less skilled, from that amount down to not more than sixty rubles a month. I found that the wages in rubles equaled our wages in dollars.

In the old industries established under the Tsarist *régime* we found the efficiency probably greater than it was in those days, but in the new plants it was not so. At the tractor plant at Kharkof, which is under construction, the workmen are not producing anywhere nearly as much. At Nizhni Novgorod, where they are building the large Ford plant to make 50,000 Fords a year, the American manager in charge of operations and consulting with the Russians told me that the carpenters were producing more than they did in America, but he asked, "How can the peasants that we call in from the fields produce in comparison with America?"

At the great agricultural machinery plant at Rostof we found the efficiency so low that from four to ten times as many machines might be bought in America for what is spent in Russia for one.

We went on to the great farms. We obtained the figures for their costs. We found that everything was piece-work, even to the plowing of the fields and the reaping and sowing of the seed. We spent a couple of days at one giant farm, motored over about 200 kilometers, and saw some 600,000 acres of virgin land. Costs are being reduced through scientific methods, although no note is taken of interest or depreciation except in machinery, which is, of course, a very large item. Managers, however, go back and forth at least once a year to America, to Canada, and to various other countries where information may be obtained.

I went down into the oil field at Baku on the Caspian Sea, and found oil being shipped out at world prices. The American professor with whom I spent a day told me that he could scratch his pen-knife anywhere and find oil, and in answer to my question whether Russia would not soon flood the world he said, "She is already flooding the world."

It seemed to me certain that the Russians were going to send out greatly increased quantities of raw materials, and it seemed to me, too, that they were going to hit America hardest of all, because we are raising and are dependent upon the export of raw commodities.

In manufactured goods I should say that it will be some time before they will be able to ship out any quantity, because the supply is so much less than the demand. The demand is enormous. There is a great scarcity of manufactured merchandise all over the country, and unless it becomes necessary, on account of the low price of raw commodities, to ship out the cruder manufactured goods that they are making there today, I believe that the Russians will not send anything out for at least five years. With their lower labor costs they can send out their cruder materials to the more backward nations to the East.

We talked freely with many people in all classes and I found, in the main, that they were determined to put this great plan through. They are under no delusions about the time it is going to take; it is simply a goal, and the whole nation is organized as it would be in war. It is an industrial war, but they are willing to make sacrifices to have better conditions and, in the main, they are willing to back their leaders to make a success of the Five Year Plan.

CHAIRMAN BLAKESLEE: I should like to read a quotation taken from one of the leading financial papers of New York a few weeks ago, and ask Mr. Creighton and Dr. Counts and Mr. Rorty if they would comment on this. This is from an American financial paper for American finance readers.

"There seems to be no reason, short of a general break-down of the system, why Russia cannot supply most of the important requirements in wheat of the world, and that soon. This prospect seems to spell black ruin for such countries as Canada, Australia and the Argentine. Russia has already disposed of all hope that the United States will ever again be able to find a profitable market abroad for any portion of its wheat crop, barring, of course, a general disaster to world wheat crops."

That leads to the question Mr. Creighton just touched on. To what extent is Soviet Russia likely to be an economic menace to the United States?

MR. CREIGHTON: I should say that in Russia today the standard of living is not over 20 per cent of what it is in America. It seems to me that if we could sit around a table with the Soviets and come to some arrangement with them regarding recognition, whereby they would keep within their country a large part of the wheat and raw materials they are today exporting—and will have to continue to export in order to pay for machinery and other imports—something might be accomplished. I did not see, in my recent trip of some 6,000 miles, any white bread excepting that which I had with some of the American engineers at Serpukhof, and that was imported from America.

If they could keep some of these raw materials that they so sorely need within their own country, and complete their plan in a more leisurely manner, they would not have to export to pay for machinery and other imports.

When we consider for what a short time they have really endeavored to compete with the outside world in manufacturing and what progress has been made during that period, we realize that in time they are bound to send out their manufactures because they are determined to make a success of their industries. I think we can safely look forward to a time when they will begin to send out goods in competition with us and with other nations of the world.

Let them complete their plan in a more leisurely fashion

and, by keeping within their country the wheat and other materials of which they are so much in need, raise their standard of living. Then when they do begin to send out their manufactured articles we shall be competing with a nation that has at least a 50 per cent standard when compared with America, rather than one as low as 20 per cent of ours, as it is today.

DR. COUNTS: I should like to agree in general with what Mr. Creighton said and to say a word concerning the standard of living in Russia. As I traveled through the Russian villages I often thought of the situation in the United States, and wondered where in America you would find a standard of living comparable to the standard of living of the Russian peasant. I think the only approach to it would be among the negroes of the far South where they live on a level very similar to the level of the Russian peasant of today.

That means that there is a tremendous domestic market for almost everything and the Russians are interested in developing that market just as rapidly as possible. They will be a menace, I think, to the extent that they feel compelled to export, just as Mr. Creighton said.

In the payment of machinery and for the services of technicians in pushing forward the present program of construction they have to export goods, and they export what they have. They will export such goods and sell at whatever rate they can get, because the value in terms of development to their country is, from their standpoint, immeasurable. If this tension between Russia and the rest of the world is moderated, I think it would be either because the Russian program succeeds, or because they secure credits from the rest of the world. If they had credits in larger amounts than they have, this tension between their system and the system of capitalism would be relieved.

Of course, whether Russia will in the end be a menace, after its system is developed, is anybody's question and anybody's answer. Nobody knows. The Russian economists maintain that under a system of socialism or collectivism exports occupy a rather different position from that which they occupy under capitalism. When they get their system established, exports will always be a function of imports. They will export only what they must, in order to supplement their own products, and to permit them to buy the things they do not or cannot produce.

COLONEL RORTY: I think that without going into an extended argument I may say that most trained economists will agree, as a matter of theory and of experience, that there is no harm done by any gradual development of international trade. It is only the sudden and violent changes in international trade which cause trouble.

Furthermore, I think they will agree that there are no international relations between wages and hours of labor, and I think they would even say what perhaps will be most astounding to the audience, that it is a matter of entire indifference to the outside world with respect to international trade whether the products of a country are produced by slave labor or by prison labor or free labor, or at high wages or low wages, or with a twelve-hour day or a six-hour day.

Astounding as those statements may be to most of you, the trained economist will generally agree that they are true, and that they are justified both by theory and experience.

I believe we can feel there is no real threat from Russia. We are concerned, not with what Russian wages are, what Russian hours of labor are, or whether the materials are produced in prison camps or not; we are concerned simply with the volume of goods sold into the international markets by Russia, and the rapidity of change in the volume of goods.

I do not believe that any Russians, selling as they must to pay for imports of machinery, are going to take a cent less for any single article of export than they can get for those exports in the world's markets. Russians are not going to sell for the pleasure of underselling. They are going to get the best prices they can for their products. I think it is a fact that the exports of wheat today are still less than the exports under the *régime* of the Tsars although they are rapidly approaching that figure and may soon surpass it.

If the change in wheat exports is a rapid one, it may cause trouble in other countries, for any rapid change in trade currents is troublesome. If it is a slow change, within the easy adjustment of the economies of the countries affected, it is not troublesome and ordinarily is not harmful.

CHAIRMAN BLAKESLEE: We have been discussing the industrial situation within Russia, and the possible economic menace from Russia. Before leaving that, may we have some comments?

M. CHARLES A. LE NEVEU, PRESIDENT OF L'UNION COLONIALE FRANÇAISE: I wonder whether, on this particular point, we are touching on the right problem. Some eight or ten years ago I had occasion to speak with one of the greatest grain merchants in this country, and, comparing facts, we discovered that the amount of wheat that this country was shipping to Europe in that and the previous year was exactly to a bushel the amount of wheat derived before the war from Roumania and Russia, which were then wiped out of the market. Therefore the question is whether you think that Russia can be obliterated permanently from the map of the world? The question is not, I think, whether Russia, with all its resources in wheat, in gold, in oil, and in unlimited fields, can be a menace to the present world.

I quite agree with Colonel Rorty that the present state of commerce is due to the fact that Russia is under a communistic system; but Russia will not be a menace, or at least will not provide any enormous change in the trade of the world.

PROFESSOR PHILIP MARSHALL BROWN, PRINCETON, N. J.: It seems to me that there is a difference of view between Colonel Rorty and Dr. Counts on the question of dumping.

I understood Dr. Counts to say that the Russians would be glad to take any price, and Colonel Rorty said no, that they will take only the best price they can get in the world markets.

I should like to make my point even more definite; take the case of timber and wood pulp, etc. Is not that process different even from dumping? Are they not really at the present moment sending their products into countries for the purpose of embarrassing capitalistic countries in this time of distress?

DR. COUNTS: I agree with the words of Colonel Rorty, if I understood him, and I think what he said is in harmony with my own remarks. The Russians will have to sell and they will take every cent they can get.

The contention that the Russians are dumping at the present time for political purposes is, I think, a myth.

PROFESSOR BROWN: I should like to ask the speaker if he thinks that when Russia is on her feet industrially, and the Five Year Plan or their present plan is worked out, the industrial power of that nation will be used for political purposes in the spreading of revolution in the world?

DR. COUNTS: I referred to that point at the close of my remarks. I said there were certain political aspects of the question. I do not care to go into them, because it is entirely a matter of speculation. Nobody knows what will happen when the present Five Year Plan and two or three other Five Year Plans are completed. Russia is moving with tremendous rapidity from the point where she is now to some other point. What her position in the world will be in fifteen or twenty years is a matter of speculation. She might use it for political purposes; she might not.

DR. HERBERT VON BECKERATH, UNIVERSITY OF BONN: Would it not be a perfectly rational thing, in view of the program of the International to spread revolution in capitalistic countries, to try at this moment, when the capitalistic countries are in distress, to embarrass them still further by sending in Russian products and hurting their industries?

DR. COUNTS: I should say, if we grant all of your premises and disregard the present situation in Russia, yes. As a matter of fact, however, the Soviet government has been tremendously embarrassed by the depression. The prices on the goods that they have shipped out are much less than what they contemplated, in fact they have been reduced by 30 per cent. The machinery that they have brought in has been brought in at a lower price, but they have gained only about 15 per cent there. That means they have had to ship out more than they intended to, and that has intensified the struggle within the country and has lowered living conditions.

DR. VON BECKERATH: May I ask another question of Dr. Counts? In order not to be misunderstood, I may say that from the point of view of Germany I would be delighted if Russia might develop, in the long run, toward a peaceful self-sufficiency. Naturally, we Germans need badly to have intense economic intercourse again with Russia. But there arises a political question which has greater importance for us than for the United States. The economic danger and distress of Germany are to a great extent undoubtedly the consequences of an intense fight between capitalistic and socialistic tendencies within Russia and Germany. As long as these fights go on, we shall always have the entirely revolutionary Communistic party in our country, even if the Russian government decides to run along on more pragmatic lines. Naturally, our Communists in Germany will always have revolutionary tendencies, and these tendencies are interrelated with the Russian government. Suppose the Russian government becomes inclined to develop along more pragmatic lines. Then these Communist leaders in Germany can say, "No, you may not do that; you will spoil our revolution in Germany." Could the Russian government, for the sake of the Russian people, simply drop its communistic ideas? I must confess some doubt about that, even though I should like to agree with Dr. Counts. I should like to hear his opinion.

DR. COUNTS: I don't know the answer, Dr. von Beckerath. I think I appreciate fully the strength of your argument. There is the international aspect of the Communist movement, and again it is anybody's guess, I suppose, as to whether the international or the national force will be the more powerful in five, ten, or fifteen years. I am inclined, in my own mind, to the view that as success is achieved, if it is achieved, on the domestic front, there will be less interest in the international movement. I think that at the present time the Soviet government is embarrassed somewhat by the claims of the Communist parties in other parts of the world that are being made upon it, but how that struggle is going to go, I do not know.

JUDGE GEORGE W. ANDERSON, BOSTON, MASSACHUSETTS: I should like to ask Colonel Rorty whether he regards individual ownership of urban values of land and subsurface rights, that is, of minerals and metals, an essential part of competitive individual capitalism?

COLONEL RORTY: I think the question of the ownership of land and natural resources is entirely separable from that of state capitalism versus individualistic capitalism. If we choose to do so, and our experience should indicate to us that it was wise to do so, it would, I believe, be entirely possible to nationalize the values of land and natural resources by taking, in the form of taxes, or depletion charges in the case of mineral deposits, the values of land and natural resources. I think that is an entirely separable problem from the problem of state capitalism and individualistic capitalism.

JUDGE ANDERSON: Then I should like to ask if these values are regarded as of common ownership, what would be the realm in which individual competitive capitalism would operate?

COLONEL RORTY: I think that the absorption of land values and the value of resources owned by the state would

not materially affect individualistic capitalism as we see it
now. The manifestations of that capitalism are primarily
in the processes of production and distribution. We use the
land as a tool, but are not in any way to depend upon private ownership of the land or natural resources.

CHAIRMAN BLAKESLEE: Here is a question from Colonel
Rorty to Dr. Counts: "How far is recognition of private
property to run in Russia?"

DR. COUNTS: I don't know. Of course, the speech by
Stalin before the Conference of Industrial Managers on
the 23rd of June represented certain concessions to capitalism. Whether those will be followed by concessions that
will permit individuals to own land, natural resources and
tools of production, I do not know. If they make a concession there, I think the revolution will be over, but I do not
think they will.

CHAIRMAN BLAKESLEE: Dr. Villari has a question for
Professor Counts: "Will the Russian peasant, closely attached as he is to the possession of a bit of land, long remain satisfied to be absorbed into a collective farm, even
if he has been educated in communism in the schools and
in the army?"

DR. COUNTS: I would say that the Russian peasant will
not remain satisfied very long, but within a generation
that peasant will have disappeared, and there will take
his place a new type of peasant, brought up under different conditions, on different ideas, with a different philosophy of life, and he may take very readily to some form of
collectivism.

CHAIRMAN BLAKESLEE: Mr. Tsurumi has a question he
would like to put to the three lecturers: "In which economic system can the sense of service as a means of preserving the existence of a community best develop?"

MR. YUSUKE TSURUMI, FORMER MEMBER OF THE JAPANESE
DIET, in explanation of his question, said: I had in mind
the present conditions in Japan which, to my mind, are
very serious. The progress of modern Japan is mostly due,

I think, not so much to the average ability of the common people of Japan as to the fortunate situation which gave us good leadership. That leadership came from the class called the Samurai, wherein men were trained to think not in terms of individual gain, but always in terms of progress of the whole community.

We are losing that class, and there is nothing to take its place. We are going through the crude system of capitalism which every nation has to go through in the beginning. Under this system, what to my mind is a very pathetic tendency is that those of the younger generation who are more aggressive and full of the acquisitive spirit, have a better chance to make material progress in life, while those of the younger generation with the spirit of the Samurai, who are thinking of the world in terms of the whole, have a tendency to be left behind.

How we can retain in this capitalistic system the old spirit of service of the class of the Samurai is a very serious problem for us and I want to learn from the three speakers, not from a religious or ethical standpoint but rather from the standpoint of self-preservation of the grade of society, which system will give more hope to sharpen the sense of self-service.

DR. VILLARI: I think that you can have developed a sense of social service under practically any system of government, provided the persons intrusted with the conduct of the government and administration are inspired by real enthusiasm for their cause.

In the case of Italy, we have had it in different periods of our history. We had it in the days of the Risorgimento, we had it in the beginnings of Fascism, and we have it at present, but whenever a system tends to become stabilized it is inevitable that that sense of enthusiasm should be somewhat attenuated. I do not think it is attendant on any particular system of government.

You have it, for instance, in England. There are a number of people who do a great deal of useful public work without any pay. It exists in other countries. I think it is rather independent of the form of government. It is more dependent on the time, on the period through which a nation is passing.

DR. COUNTS: I think that undoubtedly the question of the period, the time, and the circumstance is an important question in determining this matter. On the other hand, I am inclined to the opinion that in a communist or a collectivist state the chances are greater that an emphasis will be placed upon service to the group, than in the more individualistic systems. In fact, I think if collectivism has a merit it lies in that direction. Russia is in a position where she is developing very rapidly and organizing her resources; she is in a position that would naturally call for the subordination of the individual to the group and the devotion of the individual to the interests of the group.

COLONEL RORTY: I think that any real answer must exclude a sense of service developed out of a spirit of religious enthusiasm, whether that be an economic religion or the Fascist religion, if you please, or even the religious enthusiasm for capitalism, if we have such a thing. I think the question is primarily to be answered in terms of a state that has passed its first enthusiasms and that is lacking in any particular religious spirit. In that case I should say that all unified societies would show that spirit of service according to the extent to which they were unified and the belief of the people that they had a system that was worthy and useful.

All societies tend to develop individuals who have the spirit of service, and the spirit of service tends to exist to a large extent through all populations when they are thoroughly integrated as societies.

DR. W. E. RAPPARD: Bolshevism is built upon Marxism, whose fundamental doctrine is historical materialism. Dr. Counts has said that if collectivism has any virtue, it is that of arousing the enthusiasm of service, which of course is a sentiment not to be explained by economic historical materialism. My question to Dr. Counts is, are the present Russian communists with whom he came in contact conscious of the disharmony between their fundamental dogma of economic materialism and that enthusiasm for disinterested service which seems to characterize the most ardent present-day Communist?

DR. COUNTS: I have talked with many Communists on that question. They argue that there is no disparity, and I think that they believe that there is not. I do not believe that their conception of economic determinism eliminates from the picture the importance of the rôle of ideas and emotions. They will argue that ideas and emotions have to have a natural and material basis in class, or in the society or in nature, but they recognize, I think, the importance of ideas. In fact, I think that their controversies with the Utopian socialists were somewhat over that point. They did not deny the efficacy of ideas; they simply insisted that ideas must grow out of and give expression to the aspirations and the conditions of a particular group.

DR. RAPPARD: Dr. Counts was good enough to say he had often argued the point with Communists. I would take it that he did not agree with them. Was he convinced?

DR. COUNTS: No.

CHAIRMAN BLAKESLEE: We have another question in which everybody in the room is interested, and upon which they probably have very strong convictions. This question is directed to Colonel Rorty: "Professor Counts in his address made a strong plea for the recognition of the Soviet government by the United States. Does Colonel Rorty believe that complete political recognition would be wise at the present time?"

COLONEL RORTY: I should hardly undertake to answer for our own State Department in this matter, but it is my impression that if the Soviet government internally and externally renounces perhaps still further its belief that the world revolution against capitalism is necessary for the success of its economic experiment, and furthermore if it gives reasonable evidences of good faith in its intent not to interfere in the internal affairs of other nations, there is no reason why it should not be recognized by this government.

DR. VILLARI: The Italian government entered into political and economic relations with the Soviet government, but it was understood that the Italian government was going to stand no nonsense in the way of political propaganda on the part of the representative of that government in Italy. Consequently there has never been any trouble whatsoever. There has been a certain amount of Communist propagandism in Italy, but it has never had anything to do with the Russian embassy or their agents in Italy. I think that if it is made quite clear to that government that it is not to interfere in the internal affairs of any country recognizing it, it is quite possible to enter into relations with it without any danger. That has been our experience, and possibly that of some other countries; not however of all countries.

CHAIRMAN BLAKESLEE: I should like to ask Mr. Creighton if he will discuss the wider topic of what should be the general attitude of America toward the Soviets.

MR. CREIGHTON: Our American manufacturers who have been doing business over there have, of course, no legal status. As I went over the country I found that while we sold $150,000,000 worth of goods there last year, we probably could have sold at least half a billion dollars worth. Our manufacturers, however, having no recognition from our government, of course are not in a position to pass larger credits than they have been passing there.

I believe, as one of the experts has just said, that if the Russians would agree to give up world communism, we should sit down with them in an effort to come to some terms whereby we could recognize the Soviet government. We talked with a great many people of all classes when going through the country and we made up our minds that they were more interested in kilowatt hours than they were in world communism. In fact, there seemed to be very few of the people with whom we talked who were at all interested in world communism. We talked with some of the leaders and asked them why they did not give it up and their reply was that they wanted to talk with our government, and that they would like to be recognized. They said, of course, in every instance that it was the party, and that it had nothing to do with the government, but of course everyone who goes there realizes that the party is the government.

I have already said that our government could probably find some way of doing business with them. Perhaps we could sell them large amounts of cotton. Perhaps we could do business with them and give them credits. In that way their plan would be completed in a more leisurely fashion and the standard of living would be increased. I think that if they would give up their idea of world communism, it would be very much to our advantage to recognize them, particularly from the business side of America today. I do not believe that more than ten millions of the 160,000,000 people are interested in world communism.

PROFESSOR BROWN: I am interested to know, from the legal side, whether, if there is a violation of a contract, there are any legal remedies in Russia?

MR. CREIGHTON: I do not know. If you mean with regard to an American manufacturer who does business there, I doubt it. I know one organization that had a concession there and was getting along very nicely until the government decided to eliminate the concessions within the country.

PROFESSOR BROWN: In that case, is it desirable to extend official recognition to a country which does not protect a contract?

MR. CREIGHTON: That would be something for our government to determine, I believe.

RABBI FOSTER: Is it not true that the great difficulty in understanding the whole situation is due to our using the same terms and having different meanings? I refer to the difference between our system and the Communistic system. They have really borrowed our technique and our terminology so far as production is concerned, but they don't mean the same thing that we mean when we use those terms.

We mean one thing by the terms brotherhood, industry, machinery, class struggle, and the like. The Russians mean something else, and we can't arrive at a common understanding until we speak the same language.

I want to conclude this observation by asking a question of Dr. Counts. Dr. Garfield told us at the opening of the lecture on Communism that he tried very hard to get a genuine Communist to address the Institute so that we might have an inside view of the situation, but that it was impossible to get one. In fact, a threat was held over any Communist party member who would come here and expose the views of the Communists and the activities of the Communists.

I want to ask Dr. Counts if there is anything to Communism, to the Communist program, that would make them afraid to let it be known what they are trying to do, and what they really are doing?

DR. COUNTS: If there is, they have kept it from me.

I do not know whether there is anything else to say in response to your question. I know of Communists who have come to this country and discussed pretty freely questions of philosophy and other matters. Just why it was impossible to get a representative of the government to come to the Institute I do not know. I am not sufficiently familiar with the internal politics of the Communist Party to answer that question. I should like to make a general comment, however, with regard to the question of recognition and world communism, etc.

I have always been a little amazed at our sensitiveness on this point, particularly in view of the fact that we have not hesitated at all to send out representatives of our culture and of our ideas and our religion to other countries of the world, and propagate those ideas, even insist that other cultures permit us to establish schools where we can teach other philosophies and undermine the philosophies of those countries. It is difficult to understand how a people that has done that consistently throughout generations should be excited over a question of a few Communists coming to the United States.

DR. HARRY A. GARFIELD, CHAIRMAN OF THE INSTITUTE: I should not like to have any misapprehension on the matter to which Rabbi Foster referred. The gentleman who wrote me did not offer any threats. He did not intimate, unless one chose to read between the lines, that there was a danger. The statement was to the effect that we might as well abandon the idea of getting anyone from Russia who expects to return there, to come to America and discuss economic or political questions with us at the Institute.

I should not wish to leave the impression that there was a threat held over such a person. What his reason was I do not know. It was not disclosed by the writer.

May I venture a query that is in my own mind. I do not address it to anyone here unless one chooses to answer. I have always supposed that it was a part of the understanding, one may almost say the unwritten law, of a country that the representatives from foreign countries accredited to us should leave domestic questions severely alone, and that interference of that kind would inevitably result in the severance of diplomatic relations, and the representative would be asked to return to his own country.

International lawyers must answer this question, but let us suppose that our government saw fit to recognize Russia. So long as Russia did nothing in this country that would interfere with our political institutions and the principles of government upon which we are founded, I suppose there would be no reason for withdrawing our friendly relations and severing diplomatic connections. But the moment that there was interference, then I should suppose that the situation would be presented that Signor Villari describes to us as the situation in Italy.

FROM THE FLOOR: I asked the Russian Foreign Office last year if anything could be done to further the relations between Russia and the United States. I am not privileged to give the substance of the reply, except to say here that no encouragement was given along the line of recognition such as has been discussed here this evening. I think that might supplement what has been said. We have been talking about the possibility of our wishing to recognize Russia. I saw no evidence of Russia wanting to be recognized by the United States, as we understand the term in international law.

PROFESSOR BROWN: Might I bring the attention of the assembly to the fact that Canada has already declared an embargo on all Russian goods. It did this because it felt that Russia was interfering in a spiritual way with religion and economically with some basic industries, such as lumber, coal, furniture and wheat.

A bill was presented by Senator Hardy of Nevada in our legislature during this last session of Congress for the embargo of Russian goods by our own country, and I believe such a bill will be again presented when Congress convenes.

Russia might be described as a capitalistic nation of the very highest point, because all of her business goes through the hands of one agency. Nothing could be more capitalistic than that, and nothing can possibly upset the world more than that one thing.

DEAN P. E. CORBETT, MCGILL UNIVERSITY: Dr. Brown ascribed the embargo to a sense of violated religious delicacy first, and afterwards to the danger of conflict with the interests of our major industries. The religious pretext was, I am sure, used as a very poor veil for the industrial interest, and a great many people in Canada, including myself, think my country was exceedingly foolish in such an effort. I may say that this embargo was enacted with the hope that Canada's example would be followed very soon by the rest of the world. There is considerable disappointment that it was not so followed.

PROFESSOR BROWN: I think there are certain things we ought to bear in mind. When Great Britain, France and Italy and other countries recognized the Soviet Government they did so under certain exigencies. England felt compelled to for economic reasons; I think Italy had very strong economic reasons for doing so. They left aside the main and legal question, the basic principles that underlie recognition.

Out of our practice have grown certain recognition principles which these nations in Europe have been compelled, I think, to ignore, but which we are not compelled to ignore.

I should like to suggest first of all that you do not recognize a government unless it gives you good evidence of its ability and of its willingness to fulfill all of its international obligations. Secondly, in the case of a specific country we ask this question: Are you willing to guarantee that our citizens, when they go to your country, will have freedom? Will they be free to trade, to engage in contracts; and if their contracts are violated, will they be protected in the courts?

Those are all questions which international law asks, and if they are answered in the negative, as in the case of Russia, there can be no recognition. Friends of mine have described recently the situation in the courts in Russia, where the practices are unrelated to any system of jurisprudence whatever. Of course, in the matter of property, there cannot be a legal system where the main thing is not recognized.

I must say, in due deference to Dr. Garfield, that it seems to me a much larger question than whether the envoys of a given country behave in a manner that is not conformable to your best interests. It is a question of whether you are willing to extend your recognition to a nation that is opposed to the whole system of international law which we are all interested in maintaining.

It seems to me that our government has acted very sensibly, very wisely and honorably, in holding to those governing principles requisite for recognition, and that we are not guided by sheer opportunism, or by a desire for mere economic gain and trade.

PROFESSOR SCOTT: Are there any civilized countries other than the United States which have not recognized Soviet Russia?

DR. RAPPARD: Switzerland.

CHAIRMAN BLAKESLEE: Dr. Villari says that Czecho-Slovakia has not recognized Russia, nor have some South American countries.

Second Conference

CHAIRMAN BLAKESLEE: Professor Calvin B. Hoover, of Duke University, has been asked to summarize briefly the outstanding traits in the three competing economic systems we are describing, that of the Soviets, of the Fascists, and the Capitalists.

PROFESSOR CALVIN HOOVER, DUKE UNIVERSITY: In July, 1914, the capitalistic system so completely dominated the economic, the social and the cultural life of men that it would be correct to refer to the then existing capitalistic system as the capitalist world civilization. For if the "backward peoples" of Asia, Africa and the islands of the sea had not been industrialized, they were nevertheless completely dominated by the industrialized and urbanized capitalist countries. The fearful shock which the war administered to the capitalist system was at least responsible for hastening the process of incubation of a completely new system. This new system was brought into the world by the October Revolution of 1917. The clash of communism with capitalism resulted in Italy in the "march on Rome" and the creation of a third system.

Karl Marx proclaimed that the classless state of socialism

was the logical and inevitable development from capitalism. It is possible that the classless state is neither logical nor inevitable, but it is nevertheless true that Socialism as it is being constructed in Russia at the present time offers abundant evidence of capitalist paternity. The Communist Party strains every nerve to copy the capitalistic technique of production and to further its development. The introduction of the mass production methods of capitalism does not wait upon the demonstrated profitability of those methods, nor is it delayed by concern for the inalienable property rights of individuals, for there are no such rights in Russia. Peasant husbandry, which in capitalist countries has doggedly resisted the introduction of capitalistic technique and organization, succumbs in Russia to the application of force without stint.

Urbanization, perhaps the most significant characteristic of capitalist civilization, goes forward in Soviet Russia at a hitherto unequaled rate. Mechanization, materialization and standardization of human beings press forward to an extent which must confound those critics who attributed these characteristics to the hegemony of our profit economy over all aspects of life. Those romanticists who quarreled with capitalism for compelling women to reënter economic life would find in Russia that the movement of women into industry had been tremendously accelerated. The sociologists who have seen urban capitalism as the cause of the decay of the family would find that progress in establishing the classless state in Russia had carried this process forward in a decade farther than it had been carried during half a century in the capitalist world.

Nevertheless, the economic, social and cultural system which is being established by the Communist Party differs in the most fundamental and radical way from our capitalist civilization. The orthodox Communist maintains that the present system in Russia is not socialism, but is only the period during which socialism is under construction. He is just as insistent, however, that the present system is not state capitalism, and in this contention he is certainly correct. When he says that socialism is in process or construction he means only that it has not yet proven feasible to introduce socialism in all its aspects. From our point of view we must certainly agree, I think, that the present order in Russia is essentially socialistic.

The destruction of the institution of private property marks the Russian system definitely as socialistic, and is the most outstanding difference between Russian Communism and American capitalism as well as between Russian Communism and Italian Fascism. Most of the other economic differences between Communism and the other two systems depend upon the non-existence of private property and the economic and cultural differences are also largely dependent upon it. There is, practically speaking, no private receipt of interest, rent or profits in Soviet Russia. In planning the economy of Soviet Russia the interests of no capitalist, landlord, or entrepreneur have to be consulted. No part of the income of the national economy has to be distributed among any of these categories. Nor does the national economy receive the services of individual capitalists, landlords or entrepreneurs, serving in these functional capacities.

Since there is no receipt of income from property, the standard of living which depended upon the receipt of this income has disappeared. There is no leisure class, nor is there the culture which a leisure class creates. Since living in Russia, whenever I see here a pleasant and comfortable home, with a servant or two, a couple of cars, and the rest of the standard of living which goes with it, in which the women of the family find their outlet for mental activity in contract bridge and teas, I remember that in a communist world all this would disappear, as well as the standards of living of a more luxurious sort. The new standard of living and of culture which comes into existence in a Communistic world is created not merely because of the conscious will of Communists to create such a way of life, but, in part at least, it is the inevitable concomitant of the destruction of private property.

Closely connected with the abolition of private property is the abolition of large salaries for executives, professional men, and technical experts. I know that when I say this you will think I am not familiar with recent events in Russia. The press has been full of Stalin's new concessions to the intelligentsia and interpretations of these concessions as new proof of the failure of socialism and of the consequent necessity for the reëstablishment of capitalism. These interpretations overlook several rather fundamental aspects of the matter. In the first place, differential payment for services is not new. It has been the practice for over a decade. Stressing it at the present time has been due to the fact that in 1929 and 1930 a spontaneous movement among the workers had set in for equalization of wages and salaries of all sorts. The continuous annual readjustment of wages in the different industries by the planning organs also had been in the direction of the equalization of wages, and the system of rationing which favored the manual worker at the expense of the brain worker had had a similar effect. The recent change merely represents the reëstablishment of wage and salary differentials which had been too rapidly broken down. The maximum amount which any technical expert or executive receives is still very low. The differential between the manual worker and the director of an enterprise does not approach the size of the differential in our capitalist economy. The narrow limit upon this differential is partially a logical result of the abolition of private property, since the largest returns to executives in the capitalist economy are usually dependent upon property rights in the corporation. It is also partially a result of the total lack of awe of the price system which Communists feel. They are no more willing that the free, competitive market price should determine the rent of ability than that it should determine the rent of land. The most which they are willing to concede in the way of wage and salary differential is the amount which is functionally necessary to call forth the service.

The changed status of women, in which women are completely and finally emerging from the home into industry, accompanied by the creation of nurseries, maternity aid, social insurance, socialized preparation and consumption of food, socialized apartment houses, and so on, represents both a profound social as well as an economic change. While the economic differences between capitalism and communism are perhaps more basic than the social, it is the social changes which call most sharply to our attention the gulf between the capitalist and the communist world. So long as a worker is tightening a screw upon a bit of machinery on an assembly line he need not be conscious of any essential difference between capitalism and socialism. It is after he emerges from the factory that he is in a different world. Even though the status of the intelligentsia in industry is markedly different from former times, the social change is the one of which they, too, are deeply conscious.

It is a part of Communist dogma that complete socialism can be established only when the classless state can come into existence. When that time comes there is to be no bourgeoisie, petty or great, no aristocracy, even no intelligentsia as a separate class. Nor will there be a separate peasant class in socialist society. There will be only workers, all working in industry, for agriculture will also have been industrialized. In the meantime, says the Communist, while the other classes are being "liquidated" or ground out of existence, the dictatorship of the proletariat is a necessity. During this period only the interests of the proletariat are to be considered. The peasantry are to be conciliated through the device of the *smychka,* until such time as they can also be liquidated. During this period of the dictatorship of the proletariat, the leadership for the dictatorship is to be furnished by the Communist Party. The tactical devices of the *smychka* and the leadership of the proletarian dictatorship by the Party are two of the most significant Leninist grafts upon Marxianism.

The merciless eradication of the former classes, which the Communists considered exploiters, is one of the most characteristic features of the present period in Soviet Russia. It raises the question of the extent to which the fear and force which characterize the present *régime* are characteristic only of the so-called transitional period of the dictatorship of the proletariat or whether they will continue to exist if ever the classless state is attained. If one applies the old adage of "As the twig is bent so the tree inclines" to cultural and social systems as well as to individuals, one is hardly convinced that the present restriction of human freedom and liberty is only temporary.

Although men would probably choose the sort of system under which they would prefer to live upon the basis of its social and cultural characteristics rather than upon the basis of comparative economic efficiency, it is probable that the critical factor which will determine the victory of the three competing systems is the latter. As long as capitalism can continue to turn out a larger product from its economy than socialism it will be able to offer a powerful resistance to Communism. As long as capitalism can continue to give a greater amount of product to the worker than can Communism, the prospect of the success of the World Revolution will be poor indeed.

The ability of the capitalist world to maintain this productive superiority is not, however, primarily a matter of engineering technique. From a purely engineering point of view the economy of Russia has fallen far short, as yet, of demonstrating its equality with the capitalistic system. We cannot help but be aware, during the present depression, that the problems of the capitalistic system are not primarily those which can be solved by a production engineer. Our critical problems are those of distribution and marketing. Whatever the cause, it is impossible to deny that, temporarily at least, our productive capacity is very much greater than our capacity to market and distribute products. Idle capital equipment and idle laborers confront us with a problem which we do not as yet know how to solve.

Our *laissez-faire* economy is in contrast with the centralized and authoritatively directed economy of Soviet Russia. This authority reaches down even to the worker at bench and lathe, and while it assures him of a job, it requires of him the sacrifice of a portion of the liberty which the worker in capitalist industry enjoys. It is a fact that this liberty is somewhat theoretical, however, and during the present period of unemployment, it may be a question as to the value of this abstract freedom to the worker. The fact that the Soviet worker has restrictions placed upon his freedom to move at pleasure from job to job does not arouse great horror in the bosom of a laborer in England, the United States or Germany, who cannot find a job.

One feature of the centralized and authoritatively regulated economic order in Russia is the planning system. I think that the nature of the Soviet planning system is often misunderstood. Its admirers have generally stressed those features of the system which are most susceptible to attack upon the basis of the record.

The great advantage of an authoritatively regulated economy is not its ability to carry on long-range planning but its ability to prevent jams in distribution and marketing. The Soviet Union is confronted with very serious problems in connection with the attempt to produce tractors at Stalingrad and harvesting combines at Rostov-on-Don, but it meets with little difficulty in marketing all the tractors, combines, coal, steel, oil, food and clothing it can produce. Nor is there any reason to think that any such difficulty will be encountered in the future. The authoritatively regulated economy of the Soviet Union has succeeded in casting out the twin devils of deficiency of purchasing power and unemployment. It is not necessary to be possessed of clairvoyant ability to pierce the mysterious veil of the future twenty years hence in order to carry on the degree of planning necessary to accomplish this, and as a consequence some of the supposed obstacles to a planned economy disappear.

It should be noted that Communism, in contradiction to either capitalism or Fascism, is international in character. It is common, I know, to speak of international capitalism. Socialists and Communists are frequently given to speaking of the plots of international capitalism. Capitalism would certainly be stronger if it actually were more international. Actually the interests of capitalistic nations are frequently mutually antagonistic. No better illustration of this is afforded than that of trade with the Soviet Union. From the point of view of world capitalism as an enemy of Communism, it would be advantageous for capitalists to join in refusing to trade with the Soviet Union. But capitalists as individuals and capitalists as nations cannot sit idly by and see other capitalists carrying on a profitable trade with Soviet Russia. Only the conflicting interests of capitalists and capitalistic countries have made it possible for the Soviet Union to have foreign trade of any size.

It is not necessary, of course, to stress the obvious nationalism of Fascism. The fundamentally international character of Communism is sometimes forgotten. I think that at the present time certain interviews of Stalin with newspaper correspondents, and the proposed pact of economic non-aggression proposed by Litvinov at Geneva have been misinterpreted as the death of the Comintern as an international factor. It is my own belief that nothing could be further from the truth. Would it not be a most extraordinary thing if, at a time when the difficulties of the capitalist world are the most serious since the war, Russian Communists should surrender the ideal of world revolution? Lack of time prevents me from adequately developing this point. It should never be forgotten that the Russian Revolution originated outside Russia. Upon the basis of the Marxian dogma the Bolsheviki overthrew one of the greatest of empires. Internationalism is one of the most fundamental of Marxian tenets. It has been taught to Russian youth and still is taught as a cardinal article of faith. Anyone who thinks that Stalin could eliminate the world revolution from the creed of Russian Communism, even if he wished, does not understand the fundamental nature of the Party. The idea that Stalin wishes to do so is largely a survival of the exploded belief that Stalin's victory over Trotsky was a victory of the Right over the Left.

It is with considerable trepidation that I attempt to compare Fascism with either of the other two competing systems for I can speak of Fascism only from the standpoint of an external observer. I have no special knowledge or information about it and in consequence I can only deal in abstractions. Anything which I may say is subject to amendment and correction by the multitude who are better informed than I.

In the first place, it seems to me that Fascism is only another form of capitalism and that it cannot be said to be attempting to remake the universe nor to be trying to construct a new civilization. In essence Fascism seems to me to be a defense mechanism of capitalism when confronted by the possibility of economic and political chaos or when in danger of being superseded by Communism. Such a possibility confronted Italy prior to the march on Rome. Italian capitalists certainly eagerly embraced Fascism as an alternative to what confronted them, even if they cannot be considered the creators of Fascism. The Fascist system, of course, means the abrogation of the system of *laissez-faire*, and we have come to think of that system as being an invariable concomitant of Capitalism, if not its very essence. In the United States we are accustomed to thinking that capitalists are more generally agreed in their opposition to "government interference in business" than in any other matter. But we need only think of our protective tariff to realize that the opposition is not to governmental interference as such, but to particular sorts of government interference.

Fascism shares with Communism its distrust and contempt of democracy. But once more it is necessary to say that there is no inseparable connection between capitalism and democracy. Capitalism can adapt itself to almost any political form without compromising its integrity. Fascism and the Communist Party represent an attempt to substitute authority for democracy. Yet in the case of both it has meant, as well, the recognition of the necessity of creating an organization which would not wield authority primarily in the private interests of the leaders of the organization. I do not think that any reasonable person can believe that the educational propaganda which is carried on in either the Fascist or Communist groups is mere play-acting, or that it is a cloak for the personal ambition of the leaders. It seems to me that the creation of enthusiasm, perhaps even of fanaticism, for some purpose other than purely private profit, is necessary if any organization is to assume so complete and detailed a control over the economic and social life of a nation as is true in either Italy or Russia. When we think of our Teapot Dome and Continental Oil cases which involved the personnel of both business and the federal government, and when we think of the corruption in our municipalities such as has been exposed in Chicago, New York and elsewhere, it is perhaps a matter of doubt whether in the United States we would dare bring about a greater centralization of power over our economic life without in some way developing a greater sense of social responsibility.

Instead of destroying the old before commencing to build a new system, Fascism attempts to preserve the existing society. I suppose the coming to power of Fascism in Italy did not involve the elevation of a different economic and social class to the control of society. Yet this was the essence of the change in Russia. In Italy the stratification of society continues to exist largely as it did before Fascism. In Italy there are still pleasant and luxurious villas. The lower classes still respect the gentleman. The master and servant relation remains. Fascism strives to restore meaning to class. It is hoped that the functional nature of classes can be resurrected. The landlord is expected to utilize his estate in the best interests of the national economy. The capitalist is no longer permitted to set wages at will, to stop and start production entirely as he likes, nor even to charge any price which he likes. He must consider the interests of the state as well as his own. If the capitalist at first eagerly embraced Fascism, he has since found it, in many cases, a stern taskmaster.

Communism finds the past wholly evil and the study of it of value only that new generations may rejoice in the release of the worker from bondage. Fascism turns to the past and glorifies it, finding therein the model to be emulated and perhaps surpassed. The rights of private property are curtailed, but in essence they are protected. Economically, Fascism has certain resemblances to state capitalism. It seems probable that thoroughgoing state capitalism could be more easily developed under a Fascist system than under almost any other.

Fascism is of particular interest as a possible means of escape from destruction for non-proletarian classes in the face of the threat of communism. I am thinking of Fascism not only in its Italian manifestation but as a possible politico-economic system capable of adoption elsewhere. Hitler offers his "Third Reich" principally as an escape from Bolshevism. Without the possibility of Communism, German nationalism would have continued to express itself as Hugenberg nationalism, with the hope of the restoration of the monarchy and the destruction of the Versailles Treaty as its policy and program. Without the threat of Communism the National Socialists would never have been able to obtain the financial support of an important bloc of German capitalists. A similar threat in any capitalist country could no doubt have the effect of calling forth similar support immediately.

During the present decade at least, the preliminary

skirmishes will be fought which will decide the question of the victory of capitalism or Communism. It is impossible to say whether or not the battle will be to the death. No one can say whether finally capitalism and Communism can manage to live side by side, after they have wearied of the struggle. The Christian and Mohammedan worlds struggled intermittently for centuries but finally came to live, if not in peace, still without conducting endless warfare. No one can say whether in the battle with Communism it will be necessary for capitalism to adopt its Fascist form if it is to survive. One cannot even say that the Fascist organizational form would certainly enable capitalism to strengthen itself. In the last analysis it will be the comparative economic strength of capitalism and Communism which will decide the issue. Fascism has yet to prove itself a superior system economically. Fascism rather accentuates than minimizes the clash of national economic interests.

In the face of such degree of economic success as Soviet Russia has achieved there can be no question of the serious situation confronting our capitalist world. Never in history has there developed as new and basically different a philosophy and system of life as modern Communism that it did not attempt to force itself on the world. It seems to be a universal human itch, whenever a new idea is developed, to insist that the other fellow accept the opportunity of profiting by it. Converting the infidel by the sword edge has not been the exclusive policy of Islam.

I am not suggesting that the Red Army is about to set forth on world conquest. I am calling attention to the fact that either a continuance or a recurrence of the present depression is a more serious matter than such depressions have ever been before to capitalism. Communism can only be a menace to capitalism if capitalism cannot solve its problems. In the face of the existence of Soviet Russia, capitalism cannot afford to allow Germany to slip into the abyss, or to permit the problem of unemployment to remain unsolved.

It is true that one reassuring feature of the present situation is that Soviet Russia would be extremely loath to engage in an unsuccessful attempt to assist a Communist revolution in any other country at this time. It is probable that the influence of Moscow with the German Communist Party is all on the side of preventing an abortive revolution. Until the industrialization of Russia has been carried further than it is at present, the Party will be most reluctant to embark on any first-class war (if it is possible to speak of a first-class war). But anyone who believes that the Russian Communist Party would see a successful revolution in Germany with regret lest it interfere with the Five Year Plan simply does not know the Party.

I do not at all relish the possibility either of wars or revolutions. I hope that our capitalist system can solve its economic problems within the framework of democratic institutions. I hope that it will be possible for Communism and capitalism to coexist peacefully. I wish I could be certain of it. If our system can maintain a wage level superior to that of Communism, if our system can offer the worker economic security, if capitalist countries can compose the economic and political differences among themselves, there is a chance for peace between the capitalist and Communist worlds. None of these things is impossible.

CHAIRMAN BLAKESLEE: Before taking up the discussion period, we are to be favored by a short paper by one of our foremost business men, who happens to be visiting the Institute at the moment and whose particular line of business makes it necessary for him to give particular attention to the Soviet economic system—Mr. W. R. Brown, Chairman of the Forestry Commission of New Hampshire, Director of the American Forestry Association, and an official of the Brown Company.

MR. W. R. BROWN: There has been so much confusion in the minds of many patriotic Americans as to the desirability of trade with and recognition of the Soviets that I would like to bring out certain aspects of the problem that appeal to me.

Officially, we refuse to recognize the present government of the U.S.S.R., a Communistic state, for the following reasons:

1. The attitude of the present rulers of the U.S.S.R. in breaking at will international agreements.

2. The failure to return adequate compensation for the property of Americans confiscated by the Soviet government after the Revolution of 1917 and debts contracted with the U.S. Government and private Americans under the Kerensky *régime*. A rough estimate places these debts at $750,000,000.

3. The subversive activities directed from Moscow against American institutions.

4. The unwillingness of the average American to recognize a small despotic minority, however successful, who exercise their rule by depriving the majority of the rights of life, liberty, religion, political recourse, freedom of labor, and every principle for which Americans stand.

Economically, however, a number of our largest industrialists seek the trade of these people in ever-enlarging volume and extending credit, that may well become embarrassing in the near future, and many of our engineers lend their services for high wages, to build up an adverse power.

I will take up some of the most common reasons for disregarding this conflict between principle and business expediency given by the industrialists and engineers: one is that America has little to fear actually from so distant and undeveloped a country, whose actions are of slight concern to busy and self-sufficient America.

While no doubt Russia is distant and undeveloped, the annoying fact is that her present wonderful economic advance started in the time of the Tsars before the World War and, while set back for a period, has now reached a higher point than ever before, and represents the great forward movement of a mighty people rich in natural resources.

I think it has been sufficiently brought out in these conferences that Russia has an enormous supply of basic commodities, that she is exporting them to secure the necessary cash to complete the Five-Year Plan at the best prices obtainable or at a lesser price which can be considered as dumping if it is continued, and that she will continue to do so from her surplus in the future. In oil she stands as one of the world's large producers and in 1933 her plan calls for the production of 21 per cent of the world's supply, much of it for export. In coal she is already competing with the best Pennsylvania anthracite, and Russian coal is to be found in many American cities today. A threatened embargo by the Canadian officials caused the coal dealers of Canada to discontinue its use there. This embargo was later amplified to include asbestos, furs, and timber of all kinds. In wheat she already produces one-quarter of the world's supply, and her 1933 program calls for the production of one-third of the world's supply. In timber supply, roughly estimated, she has doubled the combined area of Canada and the United States and has available for cutting at the present moment as much as all of the timber in North America. Lumber and pulpwood from this area are being shipped from her ports to all parts of the world, and are competing at home with such natural wood-producing countries as Germany, Sweden, Norway, Finland, Czecho-Slovakia, and the United States. In 1930 Russia's production of lumber was one-third of that of United States and in 1933 Russia's plan calls for two-thirds of our production, much of it for export. As an American exponent of forestry practice, I wish to bring out that forest cultivation rests on at least a fair degree of sustained value in improved woodland, and it would not be an encouraging future to look forward to—as in New York State, for instance, where it is planned to spend two millions a year for ten years in planting up the Adirondacks—if an unlimited competition may be expected for many years to come from Russia's primeval forests and low-priced timber.

In Eastern Canada it is significant that this year the English market for lumber has been largely wiped out by the English purchase of a billion and a quarter of Russian deals. Entering United States markets at the present time also are matches, furs, fish, fruits, candy, manganese, and other products.

While it is true that in manufactured products, Russia may have a home market of her own for years to come, other nations can manufacture many articles out of her cheap raw materials and compete in our markets, and are actually doing so.

An embargo, tariff, or other form of relief, should therefore include goods manufactured in whole or in part from Russian goods. It takes but a small percentage of low-priced goods in any market to bring down the price of the whole to the same level, and Russia has now the opportunity, by introducing small amounts of goods abroad at cheap prices, produced from her tax-free raw materials and by incredibly cheap labor, to drive down foreign values to a point where the standards of living are affected. By so doing she can also upset the course of trade between nations and drive a wedge of mutual dissatisfaction between them.

I feel that to meet such a situation successfully will require much coöperation between nations who have a reasonable scale of living to maintain, as ultimately living conditions determine the scale of civilization, material, intellectual, and moral. Many claim that an unscientific system will fall by its own error if sufficient light is introduced by the more civilized nations outside. My nephew, Wentworth Brown, found in his conversation with Russians that the only subject which they would not discuss was the scientific tenability of Marx theories. In these they expressed a fanatical and blind faith. This is not surprising when it is considered that now for thirteen years youth has been educated daily to accept this doctrine and has had no opportunity whatever to hear the other side. These youth are the coming rulers of the country and it will be many years before foreign contacts will be made. The intent of the Russian rulers to overthrow the so-called capitalistic nations and spread Communism to all has been recently confirmed by Ex-Governor Baxter of Maine, who has just returned from his third trip to that country.

Far from failing, as freely predicted, the Soviet *régime* has steadily gained in power since its inception thirteen years ago. The parties of protest have been successfully killed off or banished. The country is being built up with stupendous rapidity. The general level of prosperity among the proletariat who hold the reins of government is better than in prewar times, their hours of work are less, their education is advancing. The cause has taken on the appeal of a great religious movement and, whether well-founded or not, will have the carrying force and life of other religious beliefs. Men in Russia have given their lives by the tens of thousands for the supposed benefit of their fellow men. They have also killed by the tens of thousands those who did not accept the same faith. Can capitalistic foreigners, should they succeed elsewhere, expect any special consideration or a more tender fate? As Trotsky said, addressing the Fifth Congress of the Russian Communist youths at Moscow, "That means, comrades, that revolution is coming in Europe as well as in America, systematically, step by step, stubbornly and with gnashing of teeth in both camps. It will be long protracted, cruel and sanguinary."

Some hold that, after all, Russians are human and will revolt in time. The chances for revolt in Russia are dwindling rather than increasing. Power is passing more and more into the hands of a few leaders or one dictator. A well-equipped army is maintained. Certain war reserves are laid by, including a portion of the wheat crop each year. As Communism flourishes best in industrial centers, a rapid enlargement of the machine-operated coöperative farm is being pushed, to negate the small independent agriculturists who make up the bulk of the nation and whose resist-

ance to parting with their time-honored possessions is most
to be feared.

In his last will and testament Nicholas Lenin said: "Ultimately one or the other must conquer. Pending this development, a number of terrible clashes between the Soviet
Republic and the Bourgeoisie States must inevitably occur."

Some hold that Russians have neither the brains nor the
initiative to compete successfully with Americans when
left to themselves. The best informed Europeans do not belittle the intellectual power and scope of the Soviet leaders
or the powers of assimilation and inventive resourcefulness
of the mass of the Russians. A brief review of their accomplishments in the past in the arts of peace and war, of
their present strides in production and their gigantic conception of the Five Year Plan is illuminating. The official
Russian book printed in English called *The Five Year
Plan* says, "The Five Year Plan is an important part of
the offensive of the Proletariat of the world against Capitalism. It is a plan tending to undermine capitalistic stabilization. It is a great plan of the World Revolution." Their
dependence on foreign skill and experience is only temporary, and in a few years they will be able not only to
cast off all foreign guidance but to offer the severest kind
of competition. We are confronted with a joint business
and political organization which controls all foreign trade
and has a home market of 150,000,000 people. Prices can
be shifted at will from one product to another to meet or
stifle competition at any point in the world. In the production of goods, they have the initial advantage of no
fixed charges for capital investment, interest, taxes, etc.,
and labor is at a low scale of living.

It has been suggested that to meet this competition our
sole hope is to "lower the costs of production by intensive
development of the machine age," which means a greater
use of machinery and coöperation in industries in technical
and engineering research and marketing. No doubt this

would be of some help to us but is not this exactly what
Russia is doing in a much more complete way? And should
we wish to go to the same standard of living and delegate
all business to the government in order to compete with
them?

In spite of the evidences of the attempted spread of Communism in America brought to light by the Fish Committee, it is undoubtedly true that America stands in no danger of a revolution. The strategy of Communism has turned
recently to demonstrating at home that Communism works.
Whatever the means employed by the leaders, if the results
are successful, they will be held up as a shining example of
the new order. Should those who have been successful in
other nations fail to treat the great mass of their people
justly, or close the door of opportunity to any, or exercise
an arbitrary power of oppression, then the eyes of the mass
will turn on Russia, and it will be said, "See! Communism
is a success, let us try it here."

Only those having a profound ignorance of, or indifference to, the fundamental tenets of the two systems, can
fail to see the eventual clash between them coming at some
future time. Whether the modern civilized world is mon-
archist, democratic, republican, or socialist, it is grounded
on the rights of the individual to life and liberty of thought
and action in the largest degree coincident with the rights
of others, to a fair start by education, to the capital that
expresses accumulated work and attainments, to political
recourse when oppressed, to a reasonable standard of living, and a chance to rise to any class of society.

Opposed to this, the Communist holds up the state alone
as the supreme good, and every individual life is to be devoted solely to the service of the state, from which he is
asked to derive all inspiration and pleasure, and from
which he receives those things that satisfy his immediate
wants, in common with all his fellow men. Arthur Meighen,
former premier of Canada, said in part, "The forces of
Lenin set out to remould the whole Russian nation, to up-

root the institutions of ages and to refashion the ways of
men. One after another of those things towards which
humanity has clung in every land and in every age has
been taken up by the roots and pitched away.''

Should we consider the imports from Sweden and other
countries made from cheap Russian raw materials, this balance would not be so large, however, and should we consider a possible diminution of our capital assets, a few
years' balance of trade would be negligible.

It is held by some that our present favorable balance of
trade is sufficient reason for recognition. The fundamental
fact as I see it, however, is that present trade is merely an
incident in the building up of an aggressive power and an
interlude to the subversion of our institutions. To quote
President Coolidge in his message to Congress on December 6, 1923, concerning the recognition of Russia, ''I do
not propose to barter away for the privilege of trade any
of the cherished rights of humanity. I do not propose to
make merchandise of any American principles.'' And to
quote Chief Justice Hughes, then Secretary of State, in a
reply to Mr. Chicherin, Soviet Commissioner of Foreign
Affairs, concerning negotiations for recognition, ''The
American Government is not proposing to barter away its
principles. Most serious is the continued propaganda to
overthrow the institutions of this country. This Government can enter into no negotiations until these efforts directed from Moscow are abandoned.''

That they are not being abandoned in America is shown
by the report of the Fish Committee. That they cannot be
abandoned is evident when one realizes that Stalin, now the
dictator of Russia, is now prominent in the Third International, the world organization pledged to spread Communism by any and all means. In the oath taken by all
members of the Red Army the second clause reads, ''In
behalf of the working class of the Soviet Union and the entire world, I pledge myself, etc.;'' and the fourth clause
runs as follows: ''And to concentrate all my action and

thought upon the great goal of the liberation of all workers.''

The program of the Sixth Congress of the Communist International held in Moscow in 1928 tells with complete frankness what their plan is. ''We Communists have no need to hide our aims. Our purpose is the absolute ultimate control of the entire civilized world. Our purpose is not to be conceived in mere words, but it is a bloodsoaked reality. It is to overthrow every existing institution which is not communistic: it is to capture all parliaments, not by evolution but by revolution, not by ballots but by bullets.''

Let us hope that, like Germany before the World War, they have made the strategic mistake of offending too many nations at one time, and that some kind of a mutual embargo or an export agreement between other nations may be agreed upon that will save civilization until their plan falls by the errors contained in it.

To my mind, the fact remains that a state of economic world war exists in Russia, in which all men are on a wartime basis, and can be conscripted for any work that suits the Government, as has recently been done to run the railroads.

The fact remains that the Soviets are by principle and interest committed to the overthrow of our form of civilization, and the present status is just an interlude.

CHAIRMAN BLAKESLEE: Now we come to the discussion period and I am sorry that we have no genuinely admitted proponent of Communism with us.

There are a number of questions on Russia that were handed in Tuesday for Professor Counts to answer and these we might take up first. We will ask Professor Hoover to answer these.

Dr. Villari asks the first question: ''Is Russian Communism likely to continue to antagonize the rest of the world by revolutionary propaganda, and does it need the conversion of other countries to Communism in order to maintain itself in Russia?''

PROFESSOR HOOVER: I consider internationalism a fundamental part of Communism. I believe that the Russian Communist leaders are entirely sincere internationalists, and they will continue to be a fundamental and basic part of Communism.

Is it necessary for the establishment of Communism in Russia that it spread elsewhere? I don't think that it is, although it is the fundamental and orthodox position of Communists that that is true. You know that Trotsky and Stalin had an argument somewhat along that line. Stalin said that Communism could be established in one country, Russia, but that it would be under constant threat until it was established elsewhere. Trotzky said it couldn't be established at all.

CHAIRMAN BLAKESLEE: The next question, also from Dr. Villari, is, "On what grounds do the Communists of Russia base their belief that the western powers are engaged in a conspiracy to attack them?"

PROFESSOR HOOVER: They base it principally on three things. The first is the experience during the Russian civil war, in which a great number of countries did help the Russian White forces. They base it also on the fact that in a great many European countries, such as Poland, France, and others, there is a "right" group which favors intervention in Russia. Such groups always stand particularly close to the military organization in those countries, and frequently are included in the governments, as a minority group, however.

It is not, of course, the official policy of any western European government to intervene in Soviet Russia, but there is always a rather vociferous group which favors it, and because the military men in general rather lean that way, the Soviet government and the Communist Party are always able to offer in evidence statements by members of such groups and military men which seem convincing to them.

Finally, and most important, the Communists expect to destroy capitalism; in fact, they are certain in their own minds that they are going to do it. Knowing that to be true, they simply cannot understand how it can be possible that the capitalist world would not unite to destroy them first.

M. CHARLES LE NEVEU, PRESIDENT OF L'UNION COLO-NIALE FRANÇAISE: I should like to ask a complementary question. Professor Hoover said that in some countries in Europe, including France, there was a party of White Russians in touch with the military party, and therefore there was occasion for the Russians to believe there might be cause for attack.

I hope that you will not feel hurt if I say that I always like to learn about my own country. I should like to have one instance of that point.

PROFESSOR HOOVER: In the case of France, as well as of all these other countries, you will observe that I did not say there was such evidence as to give them grounds for their belief. I have only said that there is such a connection as to produce in the minds of the Communists them-selves the belief that there is reason for attack. I am not attempting to prove that there is any danger of such inter-vention. I can merely quote from the things which the Russians say. Almost any day you will read in their news-papers a story that on a certain day the representatives of some White Russian military organization marched to L'Etoile and left a wreath, or something of the sort, and that they carried the flags of the old Russian monarchy; and this is construed as evidence that France is really favorable to the Whites.

They make claims also that there is in Paris an associa-tion of White Russians, the industrial group that they never refer to, and they say it is plotting with French militarists for intervention.

I am calling your attention once more to the fact that I am by no means saying that there is actual evidence of that, but only evidences of a situation which the Communists themselves consider as sufficient.

CHAIRMAN BLAKESLEE: Tell us about the Russian firing

squad as a factor in the Communistic system. Approximately how many have been killed? What offenses are punished?

PROFESSOR HOOVER: Of course, it is quite impossible to say how many people have been killed, and it depends upon what period you are talking about. I suppose in asking the question you referred particularly to the last year or two. I think during the time when I was in Russia, a period of nine months in 1930, that from the Russian metropolitan press you could not have found references to more than perhaps a couple of hundred people who officially had been shot for counter-revolutionary activity. However, there is no doubt that the number was very much larger than that, and I would certainly put it up in the thousands. That is not merely a wild conjecture, because anyone who was living in Russia at that time and had contact with Russians knew of cases of individuals who were shot and those facts were not reported in the press.

I do not wish to leave the impression for a moment that the *régime* in Russia depends entirely upon the firing squad. It is an extremely important factor, it is true, but by no means the only one.

DR. RAPPARD: I should like to ask Mr. Hoover's opinion of a very vague but essentially important point. What does he think of the good faith of those who make public opinion on international relations in Russia? We are always told that the Communists convince themselves. I cannot imagine that the people on top, who have access to the real information, should share the opinions which they apparently spread abroad among their faithful. Has Mr. Hoover any opinions or information or impressions as to the policy pursued by Stalin and his intimates, concerning methods of making Soviet opinion on foreign relations?

PROFESSOR HOOVER: That is a very good question, and it is one that requires a very subtle answer. The situation is not at all easy to explain.

First, I will say, in regard to the possibilities of foreign intervention, that the Communists really sincerely believe

in it. I was in Russia in the spring of 1930—the most difficult period which the Soviet Union has had, I think, since
the famine. The Communist Party was absolutely convinced that there was the greatest possibility of intervention at that time. There were signs around the department
stores and everywhere, imploring people to join the Society
for Chemical Warfare and Aviation, in the face of a threat
of intervention. They thought that very likely this would
be in the shape of a Roumanian and Polish Army with a
French General Staff.

DR. RAPPARD: Who thought it?

PROFESSOR HOOVER: I have never had any personal conversation with Stalin or any of those people, but I have
discussed the matter with the small group of foreigners
there at that time, Americans, some Germans, and Russians, and they, I think, were pretty nearly all in agreement. They really believed it, and because that was the first
year I spent in Russia I almost believed it myself. One
thing acted to convince both myself and the Communists,
and that was the immensely difficult situation that the
Soviet Union found itself in. At that time there were
peasant troubles all over Russia. The food situation was
extremely bad. With these conditions and knowing what the
Communists knew, the logic of it appealed to me that here
was an opportunity, and I think the best the capitalist
world will ever have, within a reasonable time, to destroy
the Soviet Union.

DR. RAPPARD: Have you any idea of the reports which
the Communist ambassadors and ministers abroad make to
Moscow? The illusion must begin somewhere.

PROFESSOR HOOVER: I cannot answer that. It is really
pretty difficult to know in detail about troop movements,
etc.

DR. VILLARI: I should like to ask Professor Hoover a
question about the religious sentiment in Russia. Some
time ago I was in London, and a high official of the British
Museum told me that the Egyptian section of the Museum,
which as you know is extremely rich in material, had re-

ceived a letter from the Soviet Government asking them what was the best way of mummifying corpses. The corpse of Lenin had been mummified in a not very satisfactory way, and they wanted to improve on it. They considered that the Egyptian section of the British Museum would be able to give them information on the subject.

That suggests that in Russia, although religion as we know it has been destroyed, there is rising again another form of religion. The Russian people are very superstitious and this kind of religion is taking the form of the worship of relics, and now the worship of the corpse of Lenin. Perhaps Professor Hoover can tell us something about it.

PROFESSOR HOOVER: I too have heard that story. Perhaps it is true. There is, to a limited extent, a sort of cult of Lenin worshipers, yet I do not think it is very important, and I do not think there is anything that we can call a religion which is taking the place of the former religion.

CHAIRMAN BLAKESLEE: Here is a question from Sir Herbert Ames: "What is the present attitude of the Soviet Government toward those who are not atheists, but who still believe in what we call religion and wish to be allowed to worship God in their own way?"

PROFESSOR HOOVER: The Soviet Government is attempting to destroy religion as rapidly as possible, and is making very considerable progress in so doing. The maximum of pressure is brought against people to crush religion out. The Soviet Government does not prevent old people who have no important place in life from going to church, but it would be impossible for anyone who had any position of importance, if he wished to hold it, to continue going to church. It would be a question only of time.

In the case of a peasant, it would probably be the deciding factor in determining whether he would be considered a *kulak*, and so on. On account of the shortness of time I cannot go further, except to say that all along the line every possible pressure is brought against religion.

DR. RAPPARD: I really think we are extraordinarily cruel

to Mr. Hoover. He must understand that we don't look on him as defending the ideas he is expounding.

This religious question interests me from the political point of view. Every possible pressure is brought upon the inhabitants of the Soviet Union to discredit religion, yet they are inhibited by something from simply preventing public worship, as they might, because they do things more drastic than that. What is the force that prevents them from stamping out religious feeling, the outward manifestations of religious worship?

PROFESSOR HOOVER: They have gone quite a way in doing that. As rapidly as possible, churches are being closed up. Why don't they close them up at once? Simply because they fear that too great a resistance would be made if it were done all at once. Instead, they bring the most powerful pressure to bear, occasionally relaxing it when the resistance becomes too strong.

DR. RAPPARD: Does the resistance come only from the old people to whom you referred?

PROFESSOR HOOVER: No, it comes also from some of the peasants, particularly from the *kulaks,* by no means rich peasants, but the peasants who oppose the Soviet Government for any reason. They pretended to be more religious to begin with, but religion has furnished a rallying point for them in their opposition to the Soviet Government. Throughout this I am only expressing my own opinion, of course. Most of the time you will not agree with me, and no doubt you are right.

MR. SYUD HOSSAIN, LECTURER AND JOURNALIST, NEW YORK CITY: I should like to ask both Dr. Rappard and Professor Hoover for a definition of religion in this connection. As I understand it, the distinction can and should be made in this connection between Religion with a capital R, and the orthodox Russian church that existed in Russia simultaneously with the Tsarist Régime.

CHAIRMAN BLAKESLEE: That might be taken up later with Dr. Rappard.

MR. A. C. DIEFFENBACH, EDITOR "THE CHRISTIAN REGIS-

TER,'' BOSTON, MASS.: I think it is very important, and it is a mistake to deal with this matter so casually and superficially. The religion to which a great many people in Russia object, the religion against which Lenin himself offered his objection, was the religion of the Greek orthodox church with all its political mechanizations. That ought to be clearly brought to mind.

As a matter of fact, I do not believe that the antipathy of the Russian people today is against religion, the essence itself. It is against the accursed abuses that the millions of peasantry suffered for centuries; that is what Lenin meant, and he was right, in my judgment.

I do not believe that any people on the face of the earth can be irreligious, and I do not believe the Russians can be. I do, however, believe they have been revolting, and I think the question of Mr. Hossain is absolutely pertinent.

CHAIRMAN BLAKESLEE: Professor Hoover, would you care to answer either the statement or the implication from Dr. Dieffenbach that the Soviets are rather favorable to unorthodox forms of religion?

PROFESSOR HOOVER: With all due respect to the gentleman, and meaning no disrespect at all, he is quite misinformed, because the Soviet Union offers the same opposition to other religions as to the Greek Orthodox, be it the Jew, Moslem, Catholic, or sectarian.

MR. WENTWORTH BROWN, THE BROWN COMPANY, BERLIN, NEW HAMPSHIRE: It might be of interest to the conference to know that when I was in Russia I talked with one of the men connected with the International Y. M. C. A. who had been over there for some time. He was down in Odessa when I saw him. In outlining the religious situation, he said the Communist government was pursuing the strategical policy at that moment of aiding the religious sects that were competing with the Greek Orthodox religion. The idea was that these sects tended to disperse the religious opposition, and as soon as they were dispersed, he said he felt quite sure the government would treat the other sects in the same manner in which it had treated the Orthodox Church.

MR. HOSSAIN: Since you have asked for a word of comment, I should like to offer it.

It seems to me that it is essential to this discussion of the attitude of the Soviets toward religion that it should be brought out that during the whole of the Tsarist period the Greek Orthodox Church was nothing more than an annex of the Tsar. Just as the Tsardom exploited the bodies of the masses of the Russians, the Orthodox Church continuously exploited the souls of the people, and the proof of that lies in the fact that the masses of Russian peasants were illiterate to an unnecessary and appalling extent. The Russian or Greek Orthodox Church was building elaborate and expensive cathedrals but was not opening schools or colleges for the peasants, and apparently the Grand Dukes and the leaders of the hierarchy happened to get along very comfortably and harmoniously until the revolution.

My sole point is that we must not make a bogey of anti-religionism in respect of the Russian situation. The people of Russia could not be expected to have any great love for a church which had neglected their fundamental need for whole centuries, and I think that fact should be recognized.

RABBI FOSTER: I have talked this matter over with an eminent authority, a great Jewish leader of Russia now in this country, and had my attention called to what the Communists put out in Russia just now as the Ten Commandments of Russian Communism against the Jewish group. The latter is a neutral group and would be a factor in the attitude of the Russian toward religion.

These Ten Commandments comprise regulations that the Russians are urged to comply with against the Jewish group on the High Holy Days. The Russians everywhere are told that they will be doing a fine piece of work if they organize picnics, walking parties and similar affairs to divert the young people from the synagogues, concentrating upon what is known as the Jewish High Holy Days.

What Mr. Hossain says I think is not altogether appropriate, because while the church was used by the Tsar and his party, independently of the political side of the church, there was something that was highly spiritual. The Russian Communist doesn't differentiate between the spiritual and the political side. The spiritual side should have been preserved, but the Communists are ruthlessly trying to exterminate religion completely.

DR. VON BECKERATH: I entirely agree with Professor Hoover that aggressive imperialism is a necessary corollary of the Communistic ideas in the government of Russia today. Their dogmatic idea is to make that a truth. They very naturally try to do away with any kind of social or cultural forces which might be able to prove the contrary. That to me seems very simple and natural.

PROFESSOR HOOVER: I think that is quite right. I have often thought of it and noticed it. I am sure it is a factor; not the only one, to be sure, but an important one.

CHAIRMAN BLAKESLEE: Don't you think Professor Hoover is entitled to a little rest now? Shall we ask Dr. Villari to take the witness chair?

Sir Herbert Ames asks the question: "To what extent is free speech and the freedom of the press at present curtailed in Fascist Italy? Is there any prospect of restrictions in these respects being removed in the near future?"

DR. VILLARI: With regard to freedom of speech, if by freedom of speech you mean freedom to talk among individuals, there is no restriction. In fact, in Italy I have talked to people of all shades of opinion, some favorable to Fascism, some opposed to Fascism, and some who regard it from a sort of objective point of view.

With regard to freedom of the press, there are restrictions, but in Italy we have experienced what a free press meant before the Fascist *régime*, and in the early years of the Fascist *régime*, when there were no restrictions. The anti-government press adopted an attitude of such violent and seditious propaganda and incitement to revolution that something had to be done to put a stop to it, and measures were taken to restrict seditious activities.

In Italy the press had reached such a state that you had on one side the pro-Fascist, which upheld everything, and on the other side the anti-Fascist, which attacked everything, without any critical judgment at all.

The freedom of the press, like the freedom of public meetings, was a question that had to be dealt with in the way it has been dealt with in Italy, because Italy is now going through a period of transformation and transition. When that period comes to an end there may be further revision of the present regulations concerning the press.

The freedom of public meetings has always been regulated in Italy by the authorities. The authorities could always, under the old *régime*, prohibit a public meeting, and they often did so. Now the thing is done with a definite criterion of political expediency, and public meetings hostile to the government are not permitted, but it is all part of this policy of building up the new state, a policy in which national discipline and national order are regarded as more important than certain forms of freedom which are to a very large extent illusory.

CHAIRMAN BLAKESLEE: Professor Calder has this question: "When the writer was in Italy in 1926 the law regulating the formation of the bodies constituting the Corporative State was promulgated, and trade unions and employees' and professional associations were apparently abolished or rendered powerless.

"As Mr. Villari stated, the first 10 per cent of any vocation or profession that became members of the new bodies were legally the dominating factor. The law showed, however, that this was not the first 10 per cent applying for membership, but the first 10 per cent of those approved by the government. In a word, it was a handpicked body and any more admitted were similarly selected from applicants, while all in the vocation or profession had to pay dues and work under the regulations of the minority 10 per cent, whether permitted to join or rejected.

"Will Mr. Villari state what modification, if any, has been made in these extraordinarily unrepresentative methods then promulgated, and what the status was of the considerable number of workers and professionals who for some years after 1926, he indicated, remained outside the corporative bodies and in these unions?"

DR. VILLARI: The 10 per cent rule was established because the number of men who accepted the trade union system was very small. I went into the details of that subject in my lecture.

Those admitted to the trade unions consisted of practically all of those who made application, excepting a very small number directly associated with revolutionary activities and propaganda. The proof of this is that in a great many of the unions practically all of the workers engaged in that particular trade and district concerned have joined the unions, and in other cases a very considerable proportion of them have done so. All over Italy now the membership of those unions runs into millions, and their numbers are increasing every day.

Those who remained outside did so, as I explained in my lecture, for a variety of reasons, one of which is that when you become a member of the union you have to pay somewhat higher fees, and naturally the workers earning small wages would prefer not to pay the higher fees.

Another reason is that the trade union idea, by which I mean both the old and the new, has been accepted in some parts of Italy to a greater extent than in others, and in some trades more than in others. For instance, in industry it was somewhat more diffused than in agriculture and in the north of Italy it was more diffused than in the south. When the new trade unions were created, the same tendency was followed as was followed when the old unions existed; that is to say, the number of men in the north who joined was larger than that of those who joined in the south, and the number of men in industry greater than that of those in agriculture.

Moreover, when the old unions existed, they were all grouped into the general confederation of labor, which could not compare proportionately with the number of members who have actually joined the new unions.

Sir Herbert Ames: How are the delegates selected?

Dr. Villari: They are chosen by the Italian General Confederation, and they are grouped in the general union of all the cities.

Sir Herbert Ames: Why, then, is there always a contestant delegation?

Dr. Villari: Because the representatives of the labor organizations from other countries are always of a socialistic trend, and they are opposed to Fascism for purely political reasons; consequently they oppose the Fascist representatives in every way that they can. They cannot, of course, oppose the representatives of the government at the League of Nations, but they may oppose representatives of Italian labor in the International Labor Office.

Also, they raise the question that labor organizations were mixed organizations comprising both employers and employees. When the Italian Fascist system was being created, there had been an idea of constituting mixed syndicates of employers and employees. The idea never materialized.

Chairman Blakeslee: Miss Hopkinson would like to have you answer this question: "In the Corporative or Functional State, wherein each citizen exercises his political rights according to his function—i.e., as farmer, carpenter, lawyer, et cetera—what place is there for the elderly men, retired from active work, and for those who live upon income from investments? Are they disfranchised?"

Dr. Villari: They can always come into some sort of association of one kind or other. It is not necessary that they should belong to a labor or professional association. They may belong to academies of art; they may be connected with the universities, or they may be persons who have retired. They are always considered as part of the organization to which they belonged before they retired.

Persons living on income may have other organizations to which they belong, such as the organization of house-holders, etc. Practically everybody is drawn in, in one way or other.

Besides that, the professional qualification is required only for the selection of the candidates, to which all the professional organizations contribute. When it comes to the actual voting, then citizens vote as citizens, and not as members of an organization. It is only in the selection of candidates that they have a part as members of the organization.

CHAIRMAN BLAKESLEE: Before we leave Italy, are there any further comments on the Italian situation?

DR. OTTO KLINEBERG, COLUMBIA UNIVERSITY: May I ask Dr. Villari to what extent, if any, university instructors and school teachers lost positions because of failure to agree with the general Fascist program?

DR. VILLARI: I know of only two or three cases of persons deprived of their positions because they took part in definitely revolutionary and seditious activity. I have heard, however, of a large number of university professors who are definitely anti-Fascist, such as a very distinguished professor of philosophy and my good friend Senator Ruffini, who continue to hold their chairs and give their lectures regularly.

MR. HOSSAIN: I should like to supplement what Dr. Villari said by saying that I heard Professor Salvemini say that the profession of liberal educationalists had been practically wiped out as a result of the intolerance of the existing *régime* in Italy.

DR. VILLARI: He would say that.

DR. RAPPARD: I should like to ask Dr. Villari whether he thinks that if his friend Senator Ruffini were here he would have given exactly the same answer concerning educationalists.

Dr. Villari: Professor Ruffini is an extremely honest man, and I have the very greatest respect for him. Naturally he takes a view different from the view I take, and he will probably consider that there is not academic freedom in Italy. I am quite sure that Professor Ruffini, if he were here, would never do what some of the other anti-Fascists have done, and speak ill of his own country abroad. He has never done that.

I remember something that he told me some time ago in Italy about a question which was to be discussed at the Institute of Intellectual Coöperation, which he attends. He said, "This particular measure is supported (or not supported, I forget which) by the Italian government. I shall therefore take the same line; although I am an anti-Fascist and oppose the present government, when I am abroad I am simply an Italian and will defend my country and my government."

Mr. Hossain: Apropos of that, is the affirmation of utterance of truth something bounded by geographical boundaries?

Dr. Villari: If it is an affirmation of truth, No; but the statements made by a good many anti-Fascists haven't the remotest connection with truth.

Chairman Blakeslee: Sir Herbert Ames has a question for Colonel Rorty: "Can a scientific method be devised for the increase or decrease of wages to conform with the changing cost of living at different periods? How would you reduce wages in the present emergency?"

Colonel Rorty: I think the answer is very simply "No." There can be no scientific method devised for the increase or decrease of wages. In the long run, wages must be determined by productivity and competitive measures of productivity. What might be an answer to your question is that in a time like the present, where prices and wages get seriously out of balance and it is obvious that some wage reductions may take place, it is safe and reasonable to reduce wages in proportion to the reduction in the cost of living, in the hope that that reduction will restore the economic balance. It represents the least we can do toward the restoration of the balance and is in the direction of not doing more than necessary as a first step.

DR. RAPPARD: On that point, has Mr. Rorty no faith whatever in index numbers relating to the cost of living?

COLONEL RORTY: I have considerable faith in them so far as indicating the limits of reasonable wage reductions is concerned.

DR. RAPPARD: Can't you have a sliding scale?

COLONEL RORTY: You cannot have a sliding method. There are shifts and changes that will only determine themselves in the free play of economic forces, but where you are making temporary quick adjustments, I think you can use the indices to avoid making serious mistakes.

SIR HERBERT AMES: I remember that when I was in Geneva the new wage schedule for the Secretariat of the League was introduced. The wages were always divided into two parts, one unchangeable, and the other varying from year to year according to the index figure. There was a proportion of the wage of each member of the Secretariat that was variable according to the cost of living in Geneva. I should like to ask Professor Rappard whether that system was continued, and whether it proved successful.

DR. RAPPARD: It has been abandoned and consolidated. It proved successful in the opinion of the employees so long as the cost of living rose and they received corresponding increases in salary. It lost popularity when the movement turned the other way.

CHAIRMAN BLAKESLEE: Miss Wambaugh has this question: "If, as appears, war on the modern scale is a menace to the capitalistic system, is it not an essential part of intelligent economic planning that all nations of any economic importance should unite not only to outlaw war, but to enforce peace? Such a plan having been made and put into operation eleven years ago by most of the nations of the world, would it not be advisable that the United States, being the most important economic power in the world, should join in this organization, rather than remain outside, constituting a menace not only to the success of the organization, but to that of the capitalistic system and to our own prosperity?"

COLONEL RORTY: I should say in general that the United States should in due time join the League of Nations. I hope that it will join the League of Nations at as early a date as public opinion can be brought around to supporting such joining. I do not think there should be any forced entry of the United States into the League without full public support first.

As an intermediate step I do believe there might be an advantage in having the present authorities authorized to support the action of the League in economic embargoes as a means of penalizing nations that take the offensive in a military way.

CHAIRMAN BLAKESLEE: Dr. Scott has this question for Colonel Rorty: "Do you think that the efficiency of the individualistic capitalism is any substitute for the social justice of the communist state?"

COLONEL RORTY: That question has two premises in it to start with, the first that the capitalistic system is efficient, and secondly, that there is social justice in the communistic system.

I am willing to accept in a partial way the assumption that the capitalistic system is efficient. As to the social justice of the communistic system, if you are dealing with pure communism, that is not social justice, and I think I will have to let my answer stand there.

CHAIRMAN BLAKESLEE: Another question to Colonel Rorty from Dr. Cross: "Mr. Rorty cited history to show that the proportion of the national income received by capital and labor was 30 per cent and 70 per cent respectively, deducing thereby the unalterable law that such a division is to be maintained indefinitely. What justification is there for such a conclusion?"

COLONEL RORTY: Dr. Cross has slightly misunderstood

what I said. I summarized my whole position on this question of the proportion of the national income which accrues to capital by saying there was a very interesting history there. In the early stages of the industrial revolution, particularly in the time of Karl Marx, there was a very rapid increase in the proportion of the value product of industry which accrued to capital. That built up steadily to about 30 per cent of the total product, and remained, perhaps, for a quarter-century, I suppose, at around 30 per cent of the value product of the industry. There is no absolute economic reason why that percentage might not go higher, but as a matter of practice it has been almost stationary for about twenty-five years, and there are pretty definite indications that it is declining slowly at the present moment.

The reasons for a decline in the percentage of the value product accruing to capital lie in the tendency of scientific business to increase the volume of business done, or the volume of services produced per dollar of invested capital. Chain stores have increased the annual volume of business done per dollar of invested capital, and if you analyze the operations of chain stores, you will find that they have increased the percentage of the value product of chain store operations accruing to labor as compared with the percentage that occurs in the ordinary type of store. The same is true in industry. My impression is that the tendency will be to reduce to about a 25 per cent figure. All we can say with any positiveness is that that ratio of 70 per cent to labor and 30 per cent to capital has not tended to increase, and there is evidence that it is tending to decline. We cannot say that there is any absolute law regarding it.

DR. RAPPARD: Is it not quite possible, in fact probable, that with the quantum of capital in a given community increasing faster than the number of laborers, you will have increasing parts of the social product going to capital, while wages rise absolutely but not relatively to the social product. Capital will be more and more widely distributed, so a great many of the laborers will receive a part of the income in the form of interest on capital. I should say that, looking at it from that angle, one could almost with certainty affirm that the part of the social product going to capital in a progressive community is bound to increase.

COLONEL RORTY: I had that conviction on this question when I began to examine it. It is a rather new thing to economists. My impression was that the percentage of the value product of industry accruing to capital might rise. I doubted and questioned the statistics which indicated that if anything it had fallen within the last quarter century, and then I began to consider it from this fundamental angle of the increasing turnover of capital, the increasing volume of business done per dollar of invested capital, and also from the standpoint of the interest charge on the machine per dollar of product.

From both angles I began to see possibilities that the percentage of the value product accruing to capital might decline, and I think that the answer to your question is that undoubtedly here in the United States, taking it as a specific case of the capitalistic system, the income per worker will constantly increase, but not as rapidly as the wages of the worker. Therefore this percentage accruing to capital of the total amount distributable between capital and labor will decline slowly, but very slowly. I should be surprised if that decline amounted to more than one or two per cent in ten years. I do believe that the percentage is stabilized at 30 per cent or less of the value product; that there is no definite tendency for it to increase; that what evidence there is, is that it will slowly decline rather than increase further.

I think that is still compatible with your thought that there will be an increase in the capital per worker.

DEAN CORBETT: I have always been rather puzzled, I confess, by Colonel Rorty's use of the word "efficiency." I do not know what it means. He tried to explain it to me in private conversation and I am still in the dark. He says that the modern capitalistic society is efficient—not as efficient as he would like it to be, but still efficient.

I should have thought that our deliberations here for the last week have been evidence of the great inefficiency of capitalist society. It seems to me that the efficiency of a social method of organization is to be measured in the welfare of a people subject to it, and it seems to me that an order that permits such distresses as our capitalistic order may scarcely be described as efficient.

What is Colonel Rorty's definition of efficiency? Is it mere productivity in goods, and what is the object of productivity in goods if it isn't social welfare, and isn't it possible that communism may offer a social welfare that is efficient?

COLONEL RORTY: I have been talking in many cases of the purely mechanical efficiency inherent in a capitalistic system, yet I have not been neglectful at all of the total efficiency, which would include the psychical element. My personal conviction is that communism is a long way from even offering anything like the benefits attributed to it. I am perfectly willing to admit that the capitalistic system has a very large job ahead of it at this moment in developing psychic benefits, if you please, to match its mechanical efficiency, and one of the big problems capitalism has is to teach its own mechanism to a people. The ruin of a capitalistic system will come not from its own defects, but from a failure of the people to understand its nature as it grows in complexity.

MR. HERBERT FEIS, AUTHOR, ECONOMIST, WASHINGTON, D.C.: I want to ask Colonel Rorty about his 30 per cent figure; whether his statistics of capital income were the Internal Revenue statistics, how he handled capital losses, whether the income included rent income, and, if so, what part included rent income.

COLONEL RORTY: These figures were not based on income tax figures. They were special studies I had made by the National Bureau of Economic Research.

MR. FEIS: Those were Internal Revenue figures.

COLONEL RORTY: Internal Revenue and others, variously interpreted. It would be a rather long story to tell how they were worked out. I am not sure I could even give it with exactness now.

As to the rental element in it, generally speaking that is not important. It was treated, I believe, in some of the analyses as an expense.

MR. JOHN C. BENNETT, AUBURN THEOLOGICAL SEMINARY, AUBURN, N. Y.: It seems to me that in all the ways Colonel Rorty has tried to defend capitalism he has neglected the fact that the evils which come from a system, whether capitalism or what, have their intensity as well as their extensiveness, and the statistical method measures only the extensiveness. I don't believe it is possible for a group like this to speak realistically of capitalism. I suggest that any group which lived closer to those who feel the burden of capitalistic systems might well come to the conclusion that any system would have to be very, very bad to be worse.

CHAIRMAN BLAKESLEE: A question to Professor Hoover from Professor Underhill: "When the first flush of enthusiasm, which seems to be semi-religious, has worn off in Russia, are not the motives which will operate among the governing few likely to be very much as in capitalistic countries? What men of energy and ambition in any society strive for is power. In our society they get power by becoming financiers or industrial captains, in Russia by rising in the ranks of the governmental machine. But in the long run, won't there always be temptation to exploit their power for their own benefit at the general expense, whatever the forms of government may be? Or does Russia provide anything in the long run which may induce a greater spirit of public service than we are likely to develop in capitalistic countries?"

PROFESSOR HOOVER: I would say that in my opinion Communism doesn't rely very much on the spirit of public service, and I am not imputing anything wrong to Communism in saying so. I am only saying one thing about

Communists, and one thing that I admire. They are realists and not sentimentalists, and they do not talk much in terms of public service. They figure that they will set up a system that makes it impossible for man to profit pecuniarily in that system. The struggle for power is there, in many ways stronger than in a capitalistic system, and it probably will always be so. I have no doubt that there will be cases where individual leaders will follow out a certain policy for their own aggrandizement, but I do not think there is much likelihood of their doing it in order to get wealth or amass property or anything of a purely pecuniary nature.

INDEX